Jeff Galloway

Running—Getting Started

Jeff Galloway

Running—

Getting Started

MEYER
& MEYER
SPORT

British Library Cataloguing in Publication Data
A catalogue record for this book is available from the British Library

Jeff Galloway – Running—Getting Started
Oxford: Meyer & Meyer Sport (UK) Ltd., 2005
ISBN 1-84126-166-1

© 2005 by Meyer & Meyer Sport (UK) Ltd.
2nd Edition, 2006
Aachen, Adelaide, Auckland, Budapest, Graz, Johannesburg,
New York, Olten (CH), Oxford, Singapore, Toronto
Member of the World
Sports Publishers' Association (WSPA)
www.w-s-p-a.org
Printed and bound by: TZ Verlag, Germany
ISBN-10: 1-84126-166-1
ISBN-13: 978-1-84126-166-9
E-Mail: verlag@m-m-sports.com
www.m-m-sports.com

CONTENTS

1   Foreword: You Can Be a Runner! 7

2   Why Run? 10

3   What You Need to Get Started 21

4   A Trip to the Running Store 28

5   Setting Yourself Up for Running Success 35

6   Your First Week—How to Begin and Continue 39

7   Your Three Week Schedule 43

8   Your Next 21 Weeks 47

9   The Galloway Run-Walk Method 56

10   Getting Physical: What Happens When We Get in
Shape 60

11   Your Journal Will Inspire You 69

12   Why Does Your Body Want to Hold Onto Fat? 77

13   Why Some People Burn a Lot More Fat 87

14   Fat Burning Training: For the Rest of Your Life 91

15   Fat Burning: The Income Side of the Equation 97

16   Good Blood Sugar = Motivation 106

17   An Exerciser's Diet 110

18   Running Form 114

19 Running Injury Free 124

20 Your First Race 129

21 Aches & Pains 141

22 Stretching 150

23 Strengthening 153

24 Staying Motivated 158

25 Cross Training: Exercise You Can Do on the
Non-Running-Days 166

26 Dealing with the Weather 172

27 Destroying Excuses 187

28 What About Kids? 191

29 What If You're Not Enjoying Your Running? 194

30 Trouble Shooting 198

31 Trouble Shooting Aches and Pains 214

32 Running After 40, 50, 60, 70 220

33 Being a Good Coach 226

34 Special Report: Heart Disease and Running 230

Photo & Illustration Credits 231

YOU CAN BE A RUNNER!

After having helped over 150,000 people make the change into the energetic lifestyle of a runner, it's clear to me that almost anyone can do this—and it doesn't have to be painful or extremely tiring. All you need to start this process is desire. Not just the desire to run, but the desire to become part of a positive process of improvement, bringing together the body, mind, and spirit.

There are few experiences in life that bestow the satisfaction we get from running and walking for an extra mile when we didn't think we could do it. According to the experts, running brings us back to our most primitive roots. It was during the long migrations of walking and running in small groups that primitive man defined and nurtured traits that are uniquely "human."

As we huff and puff up a hill toward home, we're probably experiencing the same feelings felt by ancestors more than one million years ago.

One of the big surprises about running is that it is pleasurable. Surely, all of us have met those who tried to run too far or too fast and had a bad experience. But, if you choose to take control over your schedule, slow down the pace, take walk breaks before you need them, and stay on the conservative side, you can avoid the negatives. It may take a few weeks to get it right, but once this happens you'll receive a treasure trove of rewards from almost every run.

The bonding and friendships that are forged on your runs are another special joy. On long runs the more appropriate term is "relationships." Practically every runner you'll meet will welcome you and help you. This can become a problem because you'll get many different points of view on just about every topic. Again, you are the captain of your ship, and can choose which of these paths to take. The information inside this book can steer you more directly to the advice that works.

Most of you start to run because something inside pushed or pulled. One of the effects of personal growth is a yearning of the psyche to search for a little challenge.

Running requires a unique mobilization of resources that we all have inside. As we confront the small struggles, we find that there is much more strength than we thought was there.

I want to invite you into the wonderful world of running, but you don't even need an invitation. When you run, you leave the rules behind, and enter a world where you can feel quite free. You can choose how you define running and how you proceed. I hope that you will, on occasion, pass the torch and invite others to join you. Speaking from experience, this provides an enhanced level of growth and satisfaction.

Even if you have your doubts, I ask you to believe that you will do this, and to get out on the roads, trails or treadmills of your world, and try. If you do this regularly, in a short time you will glow inside as you realize that you are connecting up with all these benefits and more. After 50 years of putting one foot in front of the other, I'm still discovering the benefits, and enjoying just about every step along the way.

This book is offered as advice to you, from one runner to another. It is not meant to be medical consultation or scientific fact. For more information in these areas, see a physician or research the medical journals. But above all, laugh and enjoy your runs.

Jeff Galloway

WHY RUN?

*"At first I needed to keep reading
about the many benefits of running—to get out the door.
Now my friends have to shut me up when I keep talking
about how great running is."*

Many scientists who study the primitive beginnings of mankind believe that before our species was clever enough to make tools and coordinate hunting strategies, our ancestors survived because they covered long distance all day, walking and running to gather food.

Competing for a limited supply in an increasingly arid climate, and lacking speed and strength, our forbearers kept moving, collecting the "leftovers" that other animals had overlooked or left behind. In the process of pushing on to the next food supply, these primitive predecessors developed the muscle adaptations to cover long distances along with a variety of psychological and spiritual rewards for their "going the distance."

So, in the eyes of many experts, mankind evolved because he was a long distance animal in—that walking and running are at the core of our being. Other specialists in primitive man believe that the covering of thousands of miles every year in small groups forced the development of human traits like cooperation and mutual support.

What is the evidence that our ancestors ran? Take the Achilles tendon. This is a marvelous mechanical unit which allows humans to move forward very efficiently and quickly, with a minimum of effort. This degree of sophistication is not needed for walking. Bio-mechanical experts believe that the Achilles evolved to its advanced design because our early ancestors ran. The proof is pointing to the fact that we were born to walk—and run.

Is running better than walking?

Walking is a great exercise which produces few injuries, while burning calories and building fitness. Once conditioned to recreational walking, one can burn many calories without realizing it. The purpose of this book is not to get walkers to switch to running. A high percentage of today's runners started as walkers, and continue to walk regularly.

- At first, the walk was a bit of a challenge to the sedentary body.
- Each walk delivered some exertion-related relaxation and inner satisfaction.
- But after several weeks or months of regular walking, the walker's improved fitness level reduced the post-walk rewards.
  - The walker inserted a few short runs into the daily walks.
    - The run segments became more frequent.
    - After the run-walk days, the walker felt better than he/she initially felt in the beginning stages of walking.
    - The walker becomes a runner.

Reasons given for running

Many walkers start running because they need to squeeze their exercise into a smaller block of time. Often this results from running into a neighbor, co-worker, family member, etc., who was wearing a running T shirt, or who was running through the neighborhood. The list of benefits from an individual will vary widely. Since I hear them every day from satisfied running "customers," the following are some of the most common:

Top reasons that walkers switch to running

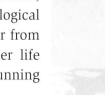

1. Running burns twice as many calories as walking the same distance.
2. Running delivers more relaxation.
3. Running controls fat much more effectively.
4. Running leaves one with a better attitude to face the rest of the day.
5. Running burns the same number of calories in about 30% of the time.
6. Running leaves one with a better dose of sustained physical energy.
7. Running bestows a greater sense of accomplishment.
8. Running gives one a sense of freedom not delivered by other activities.

As you begin to run, you will discover a wide range of positive feelings and experiences from body, mind and spirit. This is your body's way of overcoming the challenges of fatigue, aches, pains, and mental doubt. As you deal with each of these, you tie into the internal strengths that have been part of the human condition from the origin of the species. The result of this "gearing up" is an afterglow. A common reaction is that the run cleanses the mind. The rewards just keep on coming, and there are few internal feelings more powerful, or more directly connected to our being than those that come from running.

Internal rewards

While the physical rewards described later are substantial, most long-time runners acknowledge that the psychological ones are unique and more powerful. Every day I hear from runners who have participated in a variety of other life activities. They tell me over and over again that running leaves them feeling better than anything else they do.

The "Runner's High"

If you expect to be swept way into euphoria after every run, you will be disappointed. A very few runners experience this, on a very few runs. For most, there is a feeling of relaxation and enhanced well being, with increased confidence. Once you get used to these subtle rewards, they become an important and powerful boost to your day.

But, don't be discouraged if you don't get your version of the runner's high every day. While a few beginning runners tap into the good feelings from the first day, most new runners, however, experience many peaks and valleys before the rewards become consistent. If a friend seems to enjoy running more than you do, just be patient and observant. By building your base of conditioning, and by fine-tuning a few elements, you can enjoy almost every run almost every day.

Endorphins

These hormones are natural pain killers. But, they have a positive psychological effect, producing a lasting boost that can last for hours after a run. When you start running, internal monitors sense there will be pain, and initiate endorphin production to manage it. Many of the good, relaxing, positive attitude effects of a run come from these natural drugs...which are totally legal.

Vitality

After a run, you should feel energized with the motivation and the awareness to cope with the challenges of the day, or a good attitude that will help you enjoy your free time. When you are running within yourself, you feel more alive, better than normal for several hours if not all day. If you don't feel this way, you need to make some corrections usually in pace or diet mentioned in later chapters.

An attitude adjustment

Of all the things people do to improve attitude, running has been shown to be the best. Attitude research on people doing a wide range of sports, hobbies, art, and other lifestyle activities have shown that runners have the highest levels of the positive factors, and the lowest levels of the low (depression) factors. After almost every run, you will come away with a better attitude if you pace yourself conservatively, and don't go too far. When in doubt, go slower at the beginning and take more walk breaks.

Achievement

Covering distance by foot gives one a sense of achievement. This is one of the simple but satisfying rewards that have been passed on by our primitive ancestors. The bottom line is that we feel better about ourselves when we have covered some distance on that day. There is even more enhanced self-esteem in pushing back your current endurance level. As you keep going further on long runs, you feel an inner glow not experienced in other life activities.

The marathon has become a major lifestyle achievement for many people. In fact, only one-tenth of one percent of the population finish one of these 26 mile events each year. By conservative training using my run-walk method, almost anyone can do it. The sense of achievement from finishing this, or any event that is a challenge for you often changes people for the better, and can last for a lifetime.

Creativity

A number of artists have told me that they run because it improves their creative response. It has been known for some time that running is one of the best ways to activate the right side of your brain—the intuitive center of creativity. When athletes get into this right brain in a game, race, match, etc., they say that they are "in the zone." You can be there, too. If you run at a level of exertion that is within your capabilities, the steady rhythm of the feet will often stimulate brain activity on this right side.

Runners often are surprised that after trying to solve a problem all day long, it is on a run that the solution seems to appear. For example, a runner at work often hits a logical wall when using the rational left side of the brain. While running, the creative right brain works quietly and subconsciously searching for a way to get done what was needed. Many experts believe that the creative resources of this side of the brain are unlimited.

Your intuition or gut instinct is engaged when you shift into the brain's right hemisphere. As you intuitively run along, you return to some primitive areas up there which have subconscious judgement capabilities, and other powers we don't usually use.

I've conditioned my right brain to entertain me. I often start with a current problem or incident I'm trying to resolve. Ten minutes later, the right brain has often taken a portion of the original thought and mixed in a personality of someone, saying the words. After about ten more minutes, there is so much mixing of images and thoughts and association mixed images that I have to laugh.

Laughing is a right brain activity, and so is the series of images. After that, the right brain can send me a mix of various images—some real and some very abstract—without any connection to anything that came before. And on many runs each year, the solution to the original problem just drops out into a conscious thought.

More productivity, less fatigue

When beginners start running, they expect to be more tired during the day. The vast majority, however, discover that the opposite is true. A run in the morning sets your mind and body for the day. You are energized, with a good attitude to deal with problems, and bounce back. Those who run during lunch hour, when they used to work through lunch, find that they are more productive on the days that they run. Some say that the run forces them to plan better. Others say that the mental boost and relaxation gives them a boost. Many say both of these are true and more.

Friendships and bonding

For thousands of generations, humans have walked and run together. During these journeys experts believe that many of the positive team-building and caring traits were developed: sharing trust, relying upon one another, and pulling one another through difficult times. These primitive instincts are revisited in almost any group run.

Even when running with one other person, you'll find yourself sharing feelings and emotions you wouldn't share when sitting down to a cozy lunch. While running, under the influence of the right brain, you can bond more closely to your running friends, than to many family members who don't understand what running means to you.

Pushing back your physical capacity for life

I regularly see runners in their 70s, 80s and 90s who don't look their age. When I look closely, the face and skin may give a general indication of age. But, the vitality, mental energy, and good attitude would indicate an age of 1-2 decades less than the chronological one.

Why is this? In the act of extending your endurance, runners maintain a positive mental state. By "flooding" themselves with endorphins, they are more relaxed and confident. By using the muscles regularly and infusing them with oxygen on the run, these senior citizens feel good, have a healthy glow about them, and are physically able to do almost anything they did in their 40s.

A greater sense of personal freedom

Many CEOs and other busy and famous people have told me that the only segments of time during the week when they feel almost totally free is when they are on a run— sometimes with others, but often by themselves.

Without a cell phone, pager, boss, or family member around, you can explore the inner parts that are YOU. Longtime runners express this freedom in many ways. This is another way that running promotes a more free way of feeling and thinking.

You are empowered

A primary mission of this book is to help you move into the rewards more directly and easily. You can use this chapter to push you out the door on those days when gravity seems to be greater. Think about the good mental feelings after the run, and you'll have a "carrot on a stick" to keep you going when you want to quit. There will be times when you'll need to apply a reward or two as a psychological salve when overall motivation goes down on the hopefully few days when inertia seems overwhelmingly against you.

The information and suggestions inside have been forged through 30 years of working with beginners, and feedback from over 150,000 of them who have become runners. The chapters that follow can significantly reduce or eliminate the negative effects of running.

Practically every human being can enjoy the many significant rewards of running. Yes, you can start being a runner now, and unlock a continuing stream of rewards which can enrich your life in more ways than I can describe in this book.

- You are pulling from resources that are inside you.
- You find yourself becoming more intuitive as the right brain kicks in.
- You feel the confidence to grapple with a problem that is not solvable.
- You find that you have more internal strength and creativity than you thought.
- This enhanced feeling carries on to other areas of life.

Running pushes you to a higher level of physical awareness, stimulating positive activity of the brain at the same time. Whatever time we have on earth, as a runner (even a part timer) you'll have an opportunity to enjoy it to the fullest.

WHAT YOU NEED TO GET STARTED

"The most important force inside you for feeling better all the time...
... is the will to get more fit."

Sure, there are "things" that can help you, and make running easier: shoes, clothing, a training journal, watches, water belts, sun glasses, etc.. As a running store owner myself, I'm very pleased that runners enjoy these items. But, my advice to beginners is to test the waters gently, while focusing 6 months ahead. In other words, don't load up on everything you could possibly need for the rest of your running life until you know you like it. Virtually everyone can feel great after and during a run, and that becomes a greater reward than anything you can buy for yourself. In the next chapter, you will see that if you maintain desire for half a year, you are likely to continue running for life, and enjoy it. But...it all starts with desire.

One of the liberating aspects of running is the minimal requirements beyond items already owned by most people. You can run from your house or office in most cases using public streets or pedestrian walkways. You can use ordinary clothing, and you don't need to invest in expensive watches or exercise equipment, and you don't need to join a club. While running with another person can be motivating, you don't have to have a partner. Most runners run alone on most of their runs.

Runners don't have to have....

- A health club
- A team of other people
- A specific time of the day
- A specific uniform
- A piece of exercise equipment
- Lessons or a "pro" to supervise
- Competitive events

You are free to
... run by yourself
... from your home, office, kids athletic field, etc.
... run when you have time to do so, day or night
... wear what you wish
... leave behind the phone, fax, beeper

Medical check

Check with your doctor's office before you start running. Just tell the doctor or head nurse that you plan to walk with a little jogging with the idea of building up to running and walking every other day. Almost every person will be given the green light. If your doctor recommends against running, ask why. Since there are so few people who cannot run if they use a liberal walk break formula, I suggest that you get a second opinion if your doctor tells you not to run. Certainly the tiny number of people who should not run have good reasons. But, the best medical advisor is the one who wants you to get physical activity, and wants to help you get out there walking and/or running because it is the most likely way that most people will exercise.

Choosing a doctor

A growing number of family practice physicians are advocates for fitness. If your doctor is not very supportive, ask the nurses in the office if there is one who might be. The doctors who are physical fitness advocates are very often more postive and energetic.

The running grapevine can help

Ask the staff at local running stores, running club members, or long-term runners. They will usually know of several doctors in your town who runners see when they have a problem.

Doctors tell me that compared with their other patients, runners tend to ask more questions, and want to keep themselves in good health. You want a doctor who will welcome this, and serve as your "health coach", someone who will work with you to avoid injury, sickness, and other health setbacks. Doctors have also told me that runners tend to have fewer bouts with sickness.

Shoes: the primary investment: usually less than $100 and more than $65

Most runners decide wisely to spend a little time on the choice of a good running shoe. After all, shoes are the only real equipment needed. The right shoe can make running easier, and reduce blisters, foot fatigue and injuries.

Because there are so many different brands with many different models, shoe shopping can be confusing. The best advice is to get the best advice. Going to a good running store, staffed by helpful and knowledgeable runners, can cut the time required, and can usually lead you to a better shoe choice than you would find for yourself. The next section of this book will serve as a guide to getting the best shoe for you.

Clothing: comfort above all

The "clothing thermometer" at the end of this book is a great guide for this area. In the summer, you want to wear light, cool clothing. During cold weather, layers are the best strategy. You don't have to have the latest techno-garments to run. On most days, an old pair of shorts and a T shirt are fine. As you get into running, you will find various outfits that make you feel better, and motivate you to get in your run even on bad weather days. It is also OK to give yourself a fashionable outfit as a "reward" for running regularly for several weeks.

A training journal

The journal is such an important component in running that I have written a chapter about it. By using it to plan ahead and then later to review mistakes, you take a major degree of control over your running future. You'll find it reinforcing to write down what you did each day, and miss that reinforcement when you skip. Be sure to read the training journal chapter, and you too, can take control over your running future.

Where to run

The best place to start is in your neighborhood especially if there are sidewalks. First priority is safety. Pick a course, that is away from car traffic, and is in a safe area where crime is unlikely. Variety can be very motivating.

Surface

With the correct amount of cushion, and the selection of the right shoes for you, pavement should not give extra shock to the legs or body. A smooth surface, dirt, or gravel path is a preferred surface. But, beware of an uneven surface, especially if you have weak ankles or foot problems.

Picking a running companion

Don't run with someone who is faster than you unless they are fully comfortable slowing down to an easy pace that is comfortable for you. It is motivating to run with someone who will go slow enough, so that you can talk. Share stories, jokes, problems if you wish, and you'll bond together in a very positive way. The friendships forged on runs can be the strongest and longest lasting if you're not huffing and puffing (or puking) from trying to run at a pace that is too fast for you.

Rewards

You'll see in the section on "Setting Yourself up for Running Success" that rewards are important at all times. But, they are crucial for most runners in the first 3-6 weeks. Be sensitive, and provide rewards that will keep you motivated, and make the running experience a better one (more comfortable shoes, clothes, etc.)

Positive reinforcement works! Treating yourself to a smoothie after a run, taking a cool dip in a pool, going out to a special restaurant after a longer run—all of these can reinforce the good habit you are establishing. Of particular benefit is having a snack within 30 minutes of the finish of a run that has about 200-300 calories containing 80% carbohydrate and 20% protein. The products Accelerade and Endurox R4 are already formulated with this ratio for your convenience, and make good rewards.

An appointment on the calendar

Write down each of your weekly runs 2 weeks in advance on your calendar. Sure, you can change if you have to. But by getting the running slot secure, you will be able to plan for your run, and make it happen. Pretend that this is an appointment with your boss, or your most important client, etc. Actually, you are your most important client!

Motivation to get out the door

There are two times when runners feel challenged to run: early in the morning and after work. In the motivation section, there are rehearsals for each of these situations. You will find it much easier to be motivated once you experience a regular series of runs that make you feel good. Yes, when you run and walk at the right pace, with the right preparation, you feel better, can relate to others better, and have more energy to enjoy the rest of the day.

Treadmills are just as good as streets

More and more runners are using treadmills for at least 50% of their runs—particularly those who have small children. It is a fact that treadmills tend to tell you that you have gone further or faster than you really have (but usually are not off by more than 10%). But, if you run on treadmill for the number of minutes assigned at the effort level you are used to (no huffing and puffing), you will get close enough to the training effect you wish. To ensure that you have run enough miles, feel free to add 10% to your assigned mileage.

Usually no need to eat before the run

Most runners don't need to eat before runs that are less than 6 miles. The only exceptions are those with diabetes or severe blood sugar problems. Many runners feel better during a run when they have enjoyed a cup of coffee about an hour before the start. Caffeine engages the central nervous system, which gets all of the systems needed for exercise up and running to capacity very quickly.

If your blood sugar is low, which often occurs in the afternoon, it helps to have a snack of about 100-200 calories about 30 minutes before the run that is composed of 80% carbohydrate and 20% protein. The Accelerade product has been very successful.

A TRIP TO THE RUNNING STORE

"I couldn't believe the difference in my running when I found a running shoe designed for my feet."

Ask several runners, particularly those who have run for 10 years or more, about the running stores in your area. You want one that has a reputation for spending time with each customer to find a shoe that will best match the shape and function of the foot. Be prepared to spend at least 45 minutes in the store.

Quality stores are often busy, and quality fitting takes time. Getting good advice can save your feet. The experienced running shoe staff can direct you toward shoes that give you a better fit, and work better on your feet. I hear from runners about every week who have purchased a "great deal", but had to use them for mowing the lawn because they didn't work on their feet.

Bring with you the most worn pair of shoes you own—walking or running

The pattern of wear on a well-used walking shoe offers dozens of clues to a running store staff person. Primarily, shoe wear reveals the way your foot rolls, which is the best indicator of how your foot functions. Shoes are made in categories, and each category is designed to support and enhance a type of pattern of the running motion.

A knowledgeable shoe store staff person can usually notice how your foot functions

...by watching you walk and run. This is a skill gained through the experience of fitting thousands of feet, and from comparing notes with other staff members who are even more experienced (daily practice in the better stores).

Give feedback

As you work with the person in the store, you need to give feedback as to how the shoe fits and feels. You want the shoe to protect your foot while usually allowing the foot to go through a natural running motion for you. Tell the staff person if there are pressure points or pains, or if it just doesn't feel right.

Reveal any injuries or foot problems

If you have had some joint issues (knee, hip, ankle) possibly caused by the motion of your foot, called over pronation (see sidebar below), you may need a shoe that protects your foot from this excess motion.

Try several shoes in the "structure" category to see which seems to feel best while helping to keep the pronation under control.

Don't try to fix your foot if it isn't broken

Even if your foot rolls excessively one way or the other, you don't necessarily need to get an over-controlling shoe. The leg and foot makes many adjustments and adaptations which keep many runners injury free—even when they have extreme motion.

Expensive shoes are often not the best for you

The most expensive shoes are usually not the best shoes for your feet. You cannot assume that high price will buy you extra protection or more miles. At the price of some of the shoes, you might expect that they will do the running for you. They won't.

If you don't have a running store in your area...

1. Look at the wear pattern on your most worn pair of walking or running shoes. Use the guide below to help you choose about 3 pairs of shoes from one of the categories below:

Floppy?
If you have the wear pattern (spots of wear, some on the inside of the forefoot) of a "floppy" or flexible foot, and have some foot or knee pain, look at a shoe that has "structure" or anti-pronation capabilities.

Rigid?
If you have a wear pattern on the outside of the forefoot of the shoe, and no wear on the inside, you probably have a rigid foot, and can choose a neutral shoe that has adequate cushion and flexibility for you as you run and walk in them.

Can't tell?
Choose shoes that are neutral or have mid range of cushion and support.

2. Run and walk on a pavement surface to compare the shoes. If you have a floppy foot, make sure that you get the support you need.

3. You want a shoe that feels natural on your foot—no pressure or aggravation—while allowing the foot to go through the range of motion needed for running.

4. Take as much time as you need before deciding.

5. If the store doesn't let you run in the shoe, go to another store.

Go by fit and not the size noted on the box of the shoe

Most runners wear a running shoe that is about 2 sizes larger than their street shoe. For example, I wear a size 10 street shoe, but run in a size 12 running model. Be open to getting the best fit—regardless of what size you see on the running shoe box.

Extra room for your toes

Your foot tends to swell during the day, so it's best to fit your shoes after noontime. Be sure to stand up in the shoe during the fitting process to measure how much extra room you have in the toe region of the shoe. Pay attention to the longest part of your feet, and leave at least half an inch.

Width issues

- Running shoes tend to be a bit wider than street shoes.
- Usually, the lacing can "snug up" the difference if your foot is a bit narrower.
- The shoe shouldn't be laced too tight around your foot because the foot swells during running and walking. On hot days, the average runner will move up one-half shoe size.
- In general, running shoes are designed to handle a certain amount of "looseness." But, if you are getting blisters when wearing a loose shoe, snug the laces.
- Several shoe companies have some shoes in widths.

Shoes for women

Women's shoes tend to be slightly narrower than those for men, and the heel is usually a bit smaller. The quality of the major running shoe brands is equal whether for men or women. But, about 25% of women runners have feet that can fit better into men's shoes. Usually the confusion comes for women who wear large sizes. The better running stores can help you make a choice in this area.

If the shoe color doesn't match your outfit, it's not the end of the world

I receive several emails every year about injuries that were produced by wearing the wrong shoe. Some of these are "fashion injuries" in which the runner picked a shoe because the color matched the outfit. Remember that there are no fashion police out there on the running trails.

Breaking in a new shoe

- Wear the new shoe around the house for a few minutes each day for a week. If you stay on carpet, and the shoe doesn't fit correctly, you can exchange it at the store. But, if you have put some wear on the shoe, dirt, etc., few stores will take it back.
- In most cases you will find that the shoe feels comfortable enough to run immediately. It is best to continue walking in the shoe, gradually allowing the foot to accommodate to the arch, the heel, the ankle pads, and to make other adjustments. If you run in the shoe too soon, blisters are often the result.
- If there are no rubbing issues on the foot when walking, you could walk in the new shoe for a gradually increasing amount. For 2-4 days.
- On the first run, just run about half a mile in the shoe. Put on your old shoes, and continue the run.
- On each successive run, increase the amount run in the new shoe for 3-4 runs. At this point, you will usually have the new shoe broken in.

How do you know when it's time to get a new shoe?

1. When you have been using a shoe for 3-4 weeks successfully, buy another pair of exactly the same model, make, size, etc. The reason for this is that the shoe companies often make significant changes, or discontinue shoe models (even successful ones) every 6-8 months.

2. Walk around the house in the new shoe for a few days.

3. After the shoe feels broken in, run the first half mile of one of your weekly runs in the new shoe, then put on the shoe that is already broken in.

4. On the "shoe break-in" day, gradually run a little more in the new shoe. Continue to do this only one day a week.

5. Several weeks later, you will notice that the new shoe offers more bounce than the old one.

6. When the old shoe doesn't offer the support you need, shift to the new pair.

7. Start breaking in a third pair.

SETTING YOURSELF UP FOR RUNNING SUCCESS

"As soon as you take responsibility
for running three days a week, and making it fun,
you will be a successful runner."

You have a great deal of control over that part of life that revolves around exercise if you choose to take charge. The way you schedule your runs, your rewards, and your challenges will significantly influence your motivation, and the number of runs you get in per week. But, you also can control how good you will feel during each run or walk, and how quickly you will recover.

There is no need to ever experience pain in a running program. But, this puts on you, the new runner, the responsibility of a slow enough pace, and frequent enough walk breaks. All of this will be explained later in this book, but you can have fun when you run—every single day if you hold yourself back, and don't spend all of the resources early.

My first bit of advice concerning motivation is to get a training journal, look ahead, and write down the three days a week you will run each week for 2-3 weeks. Be sure to pick a time when the temperature is OK for you, and a time period when you should have open time. Lock it in! The commitment to yourself to simply get out there 3 times a week will be reinforced significantly by writing it down.

The final link in the motivational chain is to run and walk on the designated days. If you wait until the spirit moves you to run, you will probably have many empty spaces in your training journal. You must also be in charge of the little things that keep the schedule filled—such as spending a few minutes a week to plan your weekly runs, and to reward yourself afterward.

- Regularity is important for the body and the mind. When you have 3 exercise-free days between runs, you start to lose some of your running conditioning and adaptations.
- Every other day is better than running 2 or 3 days in a row. The running muscles will rebuild and rebound more quickly, and you'll find yourself wanting to get out there. Also, your mind and spirit are more likely to pull you out on your next run if you schedule every second day.
- You don't have to use a running specialized training journal. A common notebook or calendar can work just as well to help you take control over your success.

Schedule your running "appointments" as if they were your most important business client—or your boss, and make sure that you show up at each appointment.

Top Priority: Enjoying the first three weeks of running

A high percentage of those who follow the schedule below for 3 weeks will continue for 6 months. So, write down your schedule, or follow the successful one below for the next 21 days. Stick to it. After running now for about half a century, I can tell you that the first 3 weeks are crucial for making running a positive habit.

Rules for each running day

1. Run at a time of the day when the weather is comfortable.
2. If the weather doesn't cooperate, have an indoor alternative: treadmill, indoor track, indoor space where running is allowed, etc.
3. No huffing and puffing is allowed. Run at a slow pace for 10-15 seconds, and walk for a minute or two.
4. As much as possible, pick a pleasing venue to run
5. Reward yourself afterward: a smoothie, another snack, running shoes, running outfit.

Once you've run for 6 months, you're hooked!

The "half year achievers" develop a positive addiction to running—and a very high percentage continue for life. In this book you will receive a schedule that lasts for 6 months. You can break this up any way you wish. Some runners like to focus on one week at a time, others a month, while others 3-6 months. Do what is motivational for you.

A special run each week...and each month

It helps most beginners to schedule a special run each week in a scenic area, or with a motivating person or group. Each month, plan to run in a local fun run or regional festive event. Don't think that these events are only for seasoned competitors. Most of the participants do this because they enjoy the experience, and want to wear the race T-shirt. Be sure to read the chapter on your first race.

Those who run for 20 years or more tend to have the following things in common:

1. They enjoy most of the miles of almost every run.
2. They take extra days off from running to recover from aches, pains, and burnout.
3. They don't let goals (and training schedules) interfere with running enjoyment.

YOUR FIRST WEEK— HOW TO BEGIN AND CONTINUE

"The most important week is your first week.—It only takes 3 runs to get started!"

It's time to learn by doing. Here is a first run instruction list that will ease you into running—a "shake down cruise" for your body.

A caffeine boost?

To get the central nervous system ready for exercise, many runners have a cup of coffee, tea, or diet drink about an hour before they run.

If your blood sugar level is low due to any reason (especially in the afternoon), eat about half of an energy bar or drink 100-200 calories of a sports drink—especially one that has about 20% protein—about 25-30 minutes before the start of the run. If you have problems with caffeine, don't use it.

Your running stride

Run with more of a shuffle: feet low to the ground, lightly touching. Don't lift your knees. In general, make it easy on yourself. For more suggestions on easier running, see the running form section of this book.

The first run

1. Put on a pair of comfortable walking shoes (running shoes if you have them).
2. Put on light, comfortable clothes—see "clothing thermometer" in this book.

Note: clothes don't have to be designed for exercise— just comfortable.

3. Walk for 3 minutes at a slow walk to warm the muscles up gently.
4. For 2 more minutes, continue to walk slowly, or increase to a normal walk pace if you wish.
5. Then alternate 5-10 seconds of running with 1-2 minutes of comfortable walking.
6. Do this for 5-10 minutes—no more.
7. Walk slowly for 5-10 minutes as a "warm down".

Warm-up:

By walking for 3 minutes, very slowly, then walking at a comfortable, but slightly faster pace for 2 minutes, you will gently move the tendons and ligaments through the necessary range of motion. At the same time, you'll send blood into the muscles, as you get the heart, lungs, and circulation system ready for gentle exertion. Your nervous system works better when you have at least 5 minutes of easy movement as a warmup. If you need more minutes of slow walking, continue walking until you feel warmed up.

What? No stretching?

That's right. I see no reason to stretch before a run, unless you have some unusual problem that has been helped by stretching. The Ilio-tibial band injury is one of these exceptions. I've found after working with over 150,000 runners through the years that stretching causes many injuries with no benefits.

Breathing—no huffing and puffing

Don't let the level of exertion get to the point that you must huff and puff. You want to be able to talk or sing as you do your walking and running. This is called the "talk test."

Warm down:

Just walk easily for 5-10 minutes. It is important that you keep walking after you do any running. Don't ever go right into the shower after running vigorously, and don't stand around immediately after exertion either. This is a stress on your heart.

The day after

The next day, after your first run, just walk easily for 10-15 minutes.

The second run

Two days after your first run, it's your "game day" again. As long as you have recovered quickly from the first run, repeat the same routine as the first time, but extend the run-walk section by 3-5 minutes. If you haven't fully recovered, walk more and run less. In other words, extend your warm up to 8 minutes of walking. Then run for 3-5 seconds, and walk slowly for 2 minutes.

Alternate

Continue to do run-walk one day, and a day of just walking the next. The time that you spend walking, on the walking only-days, could be extended 5 minutes each day. As long as the legs and body are recovering, you could continue increasing the run-walk segment by an additional 3-5 minutes until the total reaches 30 minutes. See the schedule that follows this chapter.

Regularity

Regularity is extremely important during the first 8 weeks. If you run, even a little, every other day, your body makes the adaptations, and starts to look forward to the experience. If you wait 3 days between runs, you start to lose the adaptations, and your body complains at the beginning of each run. Getting into a habit is the most helpful way to make it past 3 weeks.

It's OK to skip some of the walk days

If you really have to leave out some of your exercise days, let them be walk days. Try to make it to each of the running "appointments."

Reward yourself!

After you have finished your first week of three sessions, congratulate yourself with a special running outfit, meal, trip to a great run-walk area, etc. Remember that rewards can be very powerful.

Congratulations! You're on your way running!

YOUR THREE WEEK SCHEDULE

"If there is any time in your life when you adjust your schedule so that you can exercise, this is it!"

If you can maintain the next three weeks of running (only 9 days of running) according to my experience, you have about an 80% chance of continuing running for 6 months. The members of the "six month club" tend to continue as life-long runners. Here are some tips for your 21 day mission:

- Find a place in your schedule when you are very likely to have time to walk and run. For most people this means getting up 40 minutes earlier. Go to bed 40 minutes earlier. But even if you don't, you can get by with 40 minutes less sleep. The overwhelming response from runners I've worked with who've said they couldn't live without those 40 minutes but tried is they really had no problem. The vitality you gain from your run will energize the rest of your day.

- Get your spouse, significant other, friends, co-workers, etc., to be your support team. Promise that if you get through the next 3 weeks having done the runs, you will have a party for them, picnic, whatever. Pick supportive people who will email you, and will be supportive during and after the training, and the celebration.

- Have a friend or three who you can call in case you have a low motivation day. Just the voice on the phone can usually get you out the door. Of course, it is always better to have a positive and enthusiastic person in this role.

- It is best to also have a back-up time to run. The usual times for this are at noon or after work.

- While commuter traffic is high, get in your run; some get to work very early, and others run immediately after work.

- If necessary, you can break up your run into several segments.

- While the walking days on Tuesday, Thursday, and Sunday will help with fat-burning and overall conditioning, these are not needed for your running improvement. If you have to spend that 20-30 minutes for family, social, or work time, take it. Even better, structure some family or social time as you walk together. There are many well-engineered strollers that are easy to push. You could also have friends go with you on a bike, etc.

Increasing the length of the run

After week two, you can increase the amount of running to between 10 and 15 seconds if you are feeling fine with this. Otherwise, just stick with 5-10 seconds. I have noted a gradual increase in the running, but cut the running portion back if you are not ready for it.

Remember, no huffing and puffing!

You will do this! Just focus on each day, and make the little adjustments that you need to make. While you are doing your runs, you can plan your 3 week success party. If you pick the right people, you may just have some converts and some companions who will join you in your mission to be a runner!

Week 2

Mission: You are continuing to increase distance. On Saturday, pick a scenic place for your run.

Mon	Tue	Wed	Thurs	Fri	Sat	Sun
15-18 min Run -Walk	walk 10-15 min	17-19 min Run -Walk	walk 13-18 min	off	18-20 min Run -Walk	15 min walk

Week 3

Mission: You're really making progress now—getting up near the half hour mark! On Saturday, ask some friends to go with you for the warm up and warm down, and have a picnic afterward. You've made it 3 weeks. Keep going, you have an easy week coming.

Mon	Tue	Wed	Thurs	Fri	Sat	Sun
20-22 min Run-Walk	walk 23-28 min	22-24 min Run-Walk	walk 26-30 min	off	24-26 min Run-Walk	30 min walk

Week 4

Mission: Rest a bit. This is an easier week to make sure the body catches up. You have earned this. It's time for your 3 week party. Pick the day, and the place, and celebrate.

Mon	Tue	Wed	Thurs	Fri	Sat	Sun
20-22 min walk	walk 20-22 min	20 min Run-Walk	walk 25 min	off	22 min Run-Walk	20 min Run-Walk

YOUR NEXT 21 WEEKS

*"You've made it through the toughest part of the program;
you only need to maintain momentum, now."*

Now that you have invested so much of yourself in the
progress and lifestyle changes, it's time to enjoy more of
your runs while focusing on the 6 month goal. Feel free to
pick a different fun activity on each week: a different
course, different person to run with, etc.

Choose your program!

Below you will find 3 programs based upon how quickly
you want to progress At the end of the chapter, you will
find a continuing program for the rest of the year.

- The Gold program is for those who have followed the schedule to date, and are feeling strong.
- The Silver program is for those who want to increase more slowly and/or have had aches and pains.
- The Fat-Burning program has more exercise time. All walks and runs should be done very slowly.

Every week, I will suggest a slight increase in the amount of running. If you don't feel comfortable with the amount of running suggested, then cut it back until it feels good.

We will start adding a cadence drill to each week after the first few weeks. You can move this drill to any day, but just try to get it in. More than any other activity, cadence drills improve your running efficiency, and ease of running while you subtly learn to run faster. This is not a workout that "hurts." In fact, most runners say that the cadence segments break up a run mentally and physically.

Cadence drill [on the Wednesdays designated by a *CD]

(1) Warm up the usual way.

(2) After about 5-10 minutes, start your drill.

(3) Time yourself for 20 seconds, and just count how many times your left foot touches. If you feel more comfortable with 10 or 15 seconds, just count for a segment of that amount.

(4) Walk for 1-2 minutes and repeat, increasing the count by 1 or 2.

(5) Repeat this 2-6 more times, attempting to increase by 1-2 in each segment.

(6) You are focusing on getting more counts. Don't try to run faster, but a slight increase might be the natural result.

(7) After the cadence drill, just finish out the time you are assigned for that day.

(8) Whatever time segment you choose (10, 15, or 20 seconds), stay with that amount.

CD denotes "cadence drill"

Gold Program

for those who have followed the schedule to date and are feeling strong

Mon.	Tue.	Wed.	Thurs.	Fri.	Sat.	Sun.

Week 5—run 15-20 seconds/walk 1-2 minutes

Mon.	Tue.	Wed.	Thurs.	Fri.	Sat.	Sun.
24-26 min Run-Walk	walk 30 min	24-26 min Run-Walk	walk 30 min	off	26-28 min Run-Walk	30 min walk

Week 6—run 15-25 seconds/walk 1-2 minutes

Mon.	Tue.	Wed.	Thurs.	Fri.	Sat.	Sun.
26-28 min Run-Walk	walk 30 min	26-28 min Run-Walk	walk 30 min	off	28-30 min Run-Walk	30 min walk

Week 7—run 20-30 seconds/walk 1-2 minutes

Mon.	Tue.	Wed.	Thurs.	Fri.	Sat.	Sun.
25 min Run-Walk	walk 25 min	23 min Run-Walk	walk 25 min	off	25 min Run-Walk	25 min walk

Week 8—run 20-30 seconds/walk 1-2 minutes

Mon.	Tue.	Wed.	Thurs.	Fri.	Sat.	Sun.
30 min Run-Walk	walk 30 min	30 min Run-Walk	walk 30 min	off	33 min Run-Walk	30 min walk

Week 9—run 25-35 seconds/walk 1-2 minutes

Mon.	Tue.	Wed.	Thurs.	Fri.	Sat.	Sun.
30 min Run-Walk	walk 30 min	33 min Run-Walk	walk 30 min	off	36 min Run-Walk	30 min walk

Week 10—run 25-35 seconds/walk 1-2 minutes

Mon.	Tue.	Wed.	Thurs.	Fri.	Sat.	Sun.
23 min Run-Walk	walk 30 min	23 min Run-Walk	walk 25 min	off	30 min Run-Walk	25 min walk

Week 11—run 30-35 seconds/walk 1-2 minutes

Mon.	Tue.	Wed.	Thurs.	Fri.	Sat.	Sun.
30 min Run-Walk	walk 30 min	30 min*CD Run-Walk	walk 30 min	off	39 min Run-Walk	30 min walk

Week 12—run 30-35 seconds/walk 1-2 minutes

Mon.	Tue.	Wed.	Thurs.	Fri.	Sat.	Sun.
30 min Run-Walk	walk 30 min	30 min*CD Run-Walk	walk 30 min	off	42 min Run-Walk	30 min walk

Week 13—run 30 seconds/walk 45-90 seconds

Mon.	Tue.	Wed.	Thurs.	Fri.	Sat.	Sun.
25 min Run-Walk	walk 30 min	25 min*CD Run-Walk	walk 30 min	off	35 min Run-Walk	25 min walk

Week 14—run 30 seconds/walk 45-90 seconds

Mon.	Tue.	Wed.	Thurs.	Fri.	Sat.	Sun.
30 min Run-Walk	walk 30 min	30 min*CD Run-Walk	walk 30 min	off	45 min Run-Walk	30 min walk

Week 15—run 30 seconds/walk 40-90 seconds

30 min Run-Walk	walk 30 min	30 min*CD Run-Walk	walk 30 min	off	48 min Run-Walk	30 min walk

Week 16—run 30 seconds/walk 40-90 seconds

25 min Run-Walk	walk 30 min	25 min*CD Run-Walk	walk 30 min	off	38 min Run-Walk	25 min walk

Week 17—run 30 seconds/walk 35-90 seconds

30 min Run-Walk	walk 30 min	30 min*CD Run-Walk	walk 30 min	off	51 min Run-Walk	30 min walk

Week 18—run 30 seconds/walk 35-90 seconds

30 min Run-Walk	walk 30 min	30 min*CD Run-Walk	walk 30 min	off	54 min Run-Walk	30 min walk

Week 19—run 30 seconds/walk 30-90 seconds

25 min Run-Walk	walk 30 min	25 min*CD Run-Walk	walk 30 min	off	41 min Run-Walk	25 min walk

Week 20—run 30 seconds/walk 30-90 seconds

30 min Run-Walk	walk 30 min	30 min*CD Run-Walk	walk 30 min	off	57 min Run-Walk	30 min walk

Week 21—run 30 seconds/walk 30-90 seconds

30 min Run-Walk	walk 30 min	30 min*CD Run-Walk	walk 30 min	off	60 min Run-Walk	30 min walk

Week 22—run 30 seconds/walk 30-90 seconds

25 min Run-Walk	walk 30 min	25 min*CD Run-Walk	walk 30 min	off	44 min Run-Walk	25 min walk

Week 23—run 30 seconds/walk 30-90 seconds

30 min Run-Walk	walk 30 min	30 min*CD Run-Walk	walk 30 min	off	60 min Run-Walk	30 min walk

Week 24—run 30 seconds/walk 30-90 seconds

30 min Run-Walk	walk 30 min	30 min*CD Run-Walk	walk 30 min	off	60 min Run-Walk	30 min walk

Week 25—run 30 seconds/walk 30-90 seconds

25 min Run-Walk	walk 30 min	25 min*CD Run-Walk	walk 30 min	off	45 min Run-Walk	25 min walk

Week 26—run 30 seconds/walk 30-90 seconds

30 min Run-Walk	walk 30 min	30 min*CD Run-Walk	walk 30 min	off	60 min Run-Walk	30 min walk

Note: Continue by alternating week # 25 and week # 26, or choose one of the training programs in *Galloway's book on Running* Second Edition: 5K, 10K or "Half-Marathon." You could also use the "beginner" marathon program in my *New Marathon* book.

Silver Program

for those who want to go a bit slower, or have had some aches and pains

	Mon.	Tue.	Wed.	Thurs.	Fri.	Sat.	Sun.
Week 5—run 10-14 seconds/walk 1-2 minutes	20 min Run-Walk	walk 22 min	20 min Run-Walk	walk 22 min	off	23 min Run-Walk	22 min walk
Week 6—-run 10-14 seconds/walk 1-2 minutes	22 min Run-Walk	walk 23 min	22 min Run-Walk	walk 23 min	off	26 min Run-Walk	23 min walk
Week 7—run 10-14 seconds/walk 1-2 minutes	16 min Run-Walk	walk 18 min	16 min Run-walk	walk 18 min	off	20 min Run-Walk	20 min walk
Week 8—run 12-16 seconds/walk 1-2 minutes	24 min Run-Walk	walk 24 min	24 min Run-Walk	walk 24 min	off	29 min Run-Walk	24 min walk
Week 9—run 12-16 seconds/walk 1-2 minutes	25 min Run-Walk	walk 25 min	25 min Run-Walk	walk 25 min	off	32 min Run-Walk	25 min walk
Week 10—run 12-16 seconds/walk 1-2 minutes	20 min Run-Walk	walk 20 min	20 min Run-Walk	walk 20 min	off	24 min Run-Walk	20 min walk
Week 11—run 14-18 seconds/walk 1-2 minutes	26 min Run-Walk	walk 26 min	26 min Run-Walk	walk 26 min	off	34 min Run-Walk	26 min walk
Week 12—run 14-18 seconds/walk 1-2 minutes	27 min Run-Walk	walk 27 min	27 min Run-Walk	walk 27 min	off	36 min Run-Walk	27 min walk
Week 13—run 14-18 seconds/walk 45-90 seconds	20 min Run-Walk	walk 20 min	20 min Run-Walk	walk 20 min	off	29 min Run-Walk	20 min walk
Week 14—run 16-18 seconds/walk 1-2 minutes	28 min Run-Walk	walk 28 min	28 min*CD Run-Walk	walk 28 min	off	38 min Run-Walk	28 min walk

Week 15—run 16-18 seconds/walk 1-2 minutes

| 29 min Run-Walk | walk 29 min | 29 min*CD Run-Walk | walk 29 min | off | 40 min Run-Walk | 29 min walk |

Week 16—run 16-18 seconds/walk 1-2 minutes

| 20 min Run-Walk | walk 20 min | 22 min*CD Run-Walk | walk 20 min | off | 31 min Run-Walk | 20 min walk |

Week 17—run 18-20 seconds/walk 1-2 minutes

| 30 min Run-Walk | walk 30 min | 30 min*CD Run-Walk | walk 30 min | off | 42 min Run-Walk | 30 min walk |

Week 18—run 18-20 seconds/walk 1-2 minutes

| 30 min Run-Walk | walk 30 min | 30 min*CD Run-Walk | walk 30 min | off | 44 min Run-Walk | 30 min walk |

Week 19—run 18-20 seconds/walk 1-2 minutes

| 20 min Run-Walk | walk 20 min | 22 min*CD Run-Walk | walk 20 min | off | 33 min Run-Walk | 20 min walk |

Week 20—run 20-22 seconds/walk1-2 minutes

| 30 min Run-Walk | walk 30 min | 30 min*CD Run-Walk | walk 30 min | off | 46 min Run-Walk | 30 min walk |

Week 21—run 20-22 seconds/walk 1-2 minutes

| 30 min Run-Walk | walk 30 min | 30 min*CD Run-Walk | walk 30 min | off | 48 min Run-Walk | 30 min walk |

Week 22—run 20-22 seconds/walk 1-2 minutes

| 22 min Run-Walk | walk 22 min | 22 min*CD Run-Walk | walk 22 min | off | 35 min Run-Walk | 22 min walk |

Week 23—run 22-24 seconds/walk 1-2 minutes

| 30 min Run-Walk | walk 30 min | 30 min*CD Run-Walk | walk 30 min | off | 50 min Run-Walk | 30 min walk |

Week 24—run 22-24 seconds/walk 1-2 minutes

| 30 min Run-Walk | walk 30 min | 30 min*CD Run-Walk | walk 30 min | off | 52 min Run-Walk | 30 min walk |

Week 25—run 22-24 seconds/walk 1-2 minutes

| 22 min Run-Walk | walk 22 min | 22 min*CD Run-Walk | walk 22 min | off | 37 min Run-Walk | 22 min walk |

Week 26—run 24-26 seconds/walk 1-2 minutes

| 30 min Run-Walk | walk 30 min | 30 min*CD Run-Walk | walk 30 min | off | 54 min Run-Walk | 30 min walk |

Note: Continue after this point alternating week # 25 and Week # 26

Fat Burning Program

The time spent walking increases significantly, so keep the pace very slow. The idea is to keep from huffing and puffing as you increase the distance covered. You can do two sessions on a day with the exception of the Saturday session. This is the long run and should be done at one time. See the fat burning chapter for more details on how more miles of easy exercise promotes fat burning.

	Mon.	Tue.	Wed.	Thurs.	Fri.	Sat.	Sun.
Week 5—run 10-12 seconds/walk 1-2 minutes	30 min Run-Walk	walk 35 min	30 min Run-Walk	walk 35 min	off	33 min Run-Walk	30min walk
Week 6—run 10-12 seconds/walk 1-2 minutes	33 min Run-Walk	walk 35 min	32 min Run-Walk	walk 35 min	off	36 min Run-Walk	33min walk
Week 7—run 10-12 seconds/walk 1-2 minutes	23 min Run-Walk	walk 25 min	23 min Run-walk	walk 25 min	off	30 min Run-Walk	25 min walk
Week 8—run 12-14 seconds/walk 1-2 minutes	33 min Run-Walk	walk 38 min	33 min Run-Walk	walk 38 min	off	40 min Run-Walk	30 min walk
Week 9—run 12-14 seconds/walk 1-2 minutes	33 min Run-Walk	walk 38 min	33 min Run-Walk	walk 38 min	off	43 min Run-Walk	30 min walk
Week 10—run 12-14 seconds/walk 1-2 minutes	23 min Run-Walk	walk 25 min	23 min Run-Walk	walk 30 min	off	33 min Run-Walk	25 min walk
Week 11—run 14-16 seconds/walk 1-2 minutes	35 min Run-Walk	walk 40 min	35 min Run-Walk	walk 40 min	off	46 min Run-Walk	32 min walk
Week 12—run 14-16 seconds/walk 1-2 minutes	35 min Run-Walk	walk 40 min	35 min Run-Walk	walk 40 min	off	49 min Run-Walk	32 min walk
Week 13—run 14-16 seconds/walk 1-2 minutes	25 min Run-Walk	walk 40 min	25 min Run-Walk	walk 40 min	off	36 min Run-Walk	25 min walk
Week 14—run 14-18 seconds/walk 1-2 minutes	36 min Run-Walk	walk 44 min	36 min Run-Walk	walk 44 min	off	51 min Run-Walk	33 min walk
Week 15—run 14-18 sec/walk 1-2 minutes	36 min Run-Walk	walk 44 min	36 min Run-Walk	walk 44 min	off	54 min Run-Walk	33 min walk

Week 16—run 14-18 seconds/walk1-2 minutes
| 25 min | walk 35 min | 25 min | walk | off | 39 min | 25 min |
| Run-Walk | | Run-Walk | 35 min | | Run-Walk | walk |

Week 17—run 14-18 seconds/walk1-2 minutes
| 37 min | walk 48 min | 37 min | walk | off | 57 min | 36 min |
| Run-Walk | | Run-Walk | 48 min | | Run-Walk | walk |

Week 18—run 15-20 seconds/walk 1-2 minutes
| 37 min | walk 48 min | 37 min | walk | off | 60 min | 36 min |
| Run-Walk | | Run-Walk | 48 min | | Run-Walk | walk |

Week 19—run 15-20 seconds/walk 1-2 minutes
| 25 min | walk 38 min | 25 min | walk | off | 42 min | 25 min |
| Run-Walk | | Run-Walk | 38 min | | Run-Walk | walk |

Week 20—run 15-20 seconds/walk1-2 minutes
| 38 min | walk 52 min | 38 min | walk | off | 60 min | 38 min |
| Run-Walk | | Run-Walk | 52 min | | Run-Walk | walk |

Week 21—run 15-20 seconds/walk 1-2 minutes
| 38 min | walk 52 min | 38 min | walk | off | 60 min | 38 min |
| Run-Walk | | Run-Walk | 52 min | | Run-Walk | walk |

Week 22—run 15-20 seconds/walk 1-2 minutes
| 25 min | walk 40 min | 25 min | walk | off | 45 min | 25 min |
| Run-Walk | | Run-Walk | 40 min | | Run-Walk | walk |

Week 23—run 15-20 seconds/walk1-2 minutes
| 40 min | walk 56 min | 40 min | walk | off | 60 min | 40 min |
| Run-Walk | | Run-Walk | 56 min | | Run-Walk | walk |

Week 24—run 15-20 seconds/walk1-2 minutes
| 40 min | walk 56 min | 40 min | walk | off | 60 min | 40 min |
| Run-Walk | | Run-Walk | 56 min | | Run-Walk | walk |

Week 25—run 15-20 seconds/walk 1-2 minutes
| 25 min | walk 42 min | 25 min | walk | off | 45 min | 25 min |
| Run-Walk | | Run-Walk | 42 min | | Run-Walk | walk |

Week 26—run 15-20 seconds/walk1-2 minutes
| 40 min | walk 60 min | 40 min | walk | off | 60 min | 40 min |
| Run-Walk | | Run-Walk | 60 min | | Run-Walk | walk |

THE GALLOWAY RUN-WALK METHOD

"The scheduled use of walk breaks gives each runner control over fatigue and running enjoyment."

One of the wonderful aspects of running is that there is no definition of a "runner" that you must live up to. There are also no rules you must follow as you do your daily run. You are the captain of your running ship, and it is you who determines how far, how fast, and how much you will run, walk, etc. Yes, running has always been a freestyle type of activity where each individual is empowered to mix and match the many variables, and come out with the running experience that he or she chooses. Walking is the most important variable for the first time runner, and can even give the veteran a chance to improve time. Here's how it works.

Walk before you get tired

Most of us, even when untrained, can walk for several miles before fatigue sets in because walking is an activity that we are bio-engineered to do for hours. Running is more work because you have to lift your body off the ground, and then absorb the shock of the landing, over and over. This is why the continuous use of the running muscles will produce fatigue, aches, and pains much more quickly. If you walk before your running muscles start to get tired, you allow the muscle to recover instantly—increasing your capacity for exercise while reducing the chance of next-day soreness.

The "method" part involves having a strategy. By using a ratio of running and walking, you will manage your fatigue. Using this fatigue-reduction tool early gives you the muscle resources, and the mental confidence to cope with any challenges that can come later. Even when you don't need the extra muscle strength and resiliency bestowed by the method, you will feel better during and after your run, and finish knowing that you could have gone further.

"The run-walk method is very simple: you run for a short segment, and then take a walk break, and keep repeating this pattern."

Walk breaks allow you to take control over fatigue in advance, so that you can enjoy every run. By taking them early and often you can feel strong, even after a run that is very long for you. Beginners will alternate very short run segments with short walks. Even elite runners find that walk breaks on long runs allow them to recover faster. There is no need to reach the end of a run feeling exhausted if you insert enough walk breaks for you on that day.

Walk Breaks
- give you control over your level of fatigue
- erase fatigue
- push back your fatigue wall
- allow for endorphins to collect during each walk break—you feel good!
- break up the distance into manageable units ("one more minute")
- speed recovery
- reduce the chance of aches, pains and injury
- allow you to feel good afterward—carrying on the rest of your day without debilitating fatigue
- give you all of the endurance of the distance of each session—without the pain
- allow older runners to recover fast, and feel as good or better than the younger days

A short and gentle walking stride

It's better to walk slowly, with a short stride. There has been some irritation of the shins when runners or walkers maintain a stride that is too long. Relax and enjoy the walk.

No need to ever eliminate the walk breaks

Some beginners assume that they must work toward the day when they don't have to take any walk breaks at all. This is up to the individual, but is not recommended. Remember that you decide what ratio of walk-run to use. There is no rule that requires you to run any ratio of run-walk on any given day. I suggest that you adjust the ratio to how you feel on a given day.

I've run for 50 years, and enjoy running more than ever because of walk breaks. Each run I take energizes my day. I would not be able to run almost every day if I didn't insert the walk breaks early and often. I start most runs taking a short walk break every minute. By 2 miles I am usually walking every 3-4 minutes. By 5 miles the ratio often goes to every 7-10 minutes. But there are days every year when I stay at 3 minutes and even a few days at 1 minute.

How to keep track of the walk breaks

There are several watches which can be set to beep when it's time to walk, and then beep again when it's time to start up again. Check our website (www.jeffgalloway.com), or a good running store for advice in this area.

How to use walk breaks

1. Start by running for 5-10 seconds, and walking 1-2 minutes.
2. If you feel good during and after the run, continue with this ratio. If not, run less until you feel good.
3. After 3-6 sessions at the ratio, add 5-10 seconds of running, maintaining the same amount of walking.
4. When you can run for 30 seconds, gradually reduce the walking time to 30 seconds, every 3-6 sessions.
5. When 30 seconds/30 seconds feels too easy, gradually increase the running time, 5-10 sec every 3-6 sessions.
6. On any given day, when you need more walking, take it. Don't ever be afraid to drop back to make the run more fun, and less tiring.

"Our bodies crave exercise, and reward us in many ways when we do so."

GETTING PHYSICAL: WHAT HAPPENS WHEN WE GET IN SHAPE

Humans are designed to improve

When we regularly perform endurance exercise, many positive changes occur inside us. I believe that this is due to the way our ancient ancestors adapted our bodies to walk and run for long distances. Assuming then that our physical design and purpose is long distance forward motion, it's no surprise that we feel so good when we do it—we are going back to our roots.

Is our body lazy?

Maybe this is too strong a statement. Let's say that our bodies want to conserve resources by doing the smallest amount of work they can get away with. If we are sedentary and never exercise, the heart slowly loses it's efficiency, deposits build up in the arteries, the lungs become less efficient because they don't have to be efficient. Only when we put these important health components to a gentle test, as in long runs, is the body forced to respond by improving in dozens of ways.

Teamwork

When called into action, the heart, lungs, muscles, tendons, central nervous system, brain, and blood system are programmed to work as a team. The right brain intuitively solves problems, manages resources, and steers us toward the many lasting health benefits resulting from running and walking.

Your leg muscles significantly help to pump blood back to the heart. By gradually extending the length of your long run, you produce very fit muscle cells. They get stronger and more efficient in moving blood in, and pushing waste produces through the system and back to the heart. Some cardiovascular experts who study the heart believe that the cumulative effect of endurance-trained leg muscles can pump significant blood flow back to the heart.

Why does long distance exercise keep the heart healthy?
Your heart is a muscle, and responds positively to endurance exercise. The slight increase in heart rate, maintained during a gradually increasing long run each week, keeps this most important muscle in shape. A strong and effective heart pumps blood more effectively not only when you exercise. Heart specialists say that this "fit" heart is more resistant to heart disease at all times.

But, if your diet is full of artery clogging foods, a strong heart will not make you immune to heart disease. A diet that is high in saturated fat and trans fat has been shown to significantly increase the chance of heart attacks, strokes, etc.

The lungs

On our long runs, the muscles demand oxygen, and must have an adequate supply to burn fat and exercise aerobically. Each muscle is like a factory composed of thousands of muscle cells who do the work. Unlike some factory workers, these are passionate and dedicated team members ready to work 24/7 to keep us moving—even when we push them too far over and over again. Running, even in short amounts, done slowly, calls them into action, stimulates them to go to exhaustion, and serves to mold them into a team.

Endorphins kill pain, make you feel good

Another important member of the team, the endorphins, manage the muscle pain and provide a positive lift.

What is endurance exercise?

The essence of endurance is to go farther—to keep doing an exercise long enough, so that the body must find more efficient ways of moving, of processing energy, sending blood, etc. For untrained muscles, a run-walk of 10 minutes will do this. As we push back this threshold, our goal is to get to 2 sessions a week of 30 minutes each, with a long one that pushes up to the current endurance limit or beyond (more than 30 minutes).

**Long one once a week pushes back
the endurance limits**

+

**Two 30 minute sessions which maintain
the adaptations gained on the long one**

=

You the endurance athlete.

Stress plus rest produces improvement

When we run and walk a little farther than we've gone in the past month or so, this gentle stress breaks down the muscle cells, tendons, etc. Our bodies are programmed to rebuild stronger than before if you have enough rest afterward (usually 48 hours), so that the rebuilding can take place.

It all starts by gently stressing the system

When we exercise about every other day, our body becomes adapted to the speed and distance currently done. To improve endurance, we start by doing a run-walk that is slightly longer than we have been doing. As you exceed the current distance limit, tired muscle fibers keep working beyond their capacity. The extra work of an additional half mile or mile may not be perceived during the longer run, but produces after-effects the next day: sore muscles, a longer time needed to feel smooth when walking, and muscles that feel tired.

Looking inside the cell, afterward, you'll see tears in the muscle cell membrane. The mitochondria (that process the energy inside the cell) are swollen. Glycogen (the energy supply needed for the first 15 minutes of exercise) is significantly reduced. There are waste products from exercise, and even bits of muscle tissue, and other after effects from a hard effort. Sometimes, breaks in the blood vessels and arteries occur with leakage of blood into the muscles.

The body rebuilds, stronger and better than before

Gentle overuse tells the body that it must improve. The damage to the muscles caused by going slightly beyond capacity is not only repaired, but the whole system is challenged to become more efficient so that more stress can be handled in the future.

If you have rested well, and look inside the cell again 2 days later, you'll see thicker cell membranes, so that they can handle more work without breaking down. The mitochondria have increased in size and number, so that they can process more energy next time. The damage to the blood system has been repaired. Waste has been removed. Over several months, after adapting to a continued series of small increases, more capilliaries (tiny fingers of the blood system) are produced, improving and expanding the delivery of oxygen and nutrients and providing a better withdrawal of waste products.

These are only some of the many adaptations that the incredible human body makes, at all levels, when we exercise: bio-mechanics, nervous system, strength, muscle efficiency and more. Psychological benefits follow the physical ones.

You are becoming part of the process of improving health and performance, which produces a positive attitude. Mind and body are connecting up for great teamwork. These are only some of the reasons why runners have been shown to be more positive people than they were before they became runners.

Quality rest is crucial: 48 hours between workouts

Without sufficient rest, the rebuilding will not proceed as quickly, or as well as it could. I'm not talking about staying in bed all day after a workout. If you have run a hard workout in the morning, you'll actually recover faster if you gently walk around the rest of the day. The day after a run, it's usually fine to perform gentle movement, as in walking. There are other options for easy days in the chapter on cross training.

The key to rebuilding stressed muscle cells is to avoid exercises that strenuously use the calf muscle (stair machines, step aerobics, spinning out of the saddle) for the 48 hour period between running workouts. If you have other aches and pains from your individual "weak links", then don't do exercises that aggravate them further. As long as you are not continuing to stress the calf, most alternative exercises are fine.

If you don't have time on the non-running days to do the alternative exercise, don't feel guilty. Cross training is not necessary for running improvement. Why do it? Well, it helps those who want to burn more fat. Also, many new runners like the way they feel after running, and want to feel that way every day. Even running 2 days in a row produces significant damage, and requires much more recovery than an every-other day run schedule. Once you find the cross training mode that works best for you, you can enjoy the post exercise glow every day.

Junk miles

Some beginners feel so good when they start a running program that they "sneak in" a few miles on the days they should be resting. They often lie to themselves, assuming that this short distance isn't really running.

The problem is that these short runs, which improve your conditioning, don't give your muscles the rest needed for maximum recovery. They are called "junk miles." It's always better to stay with a 48 hour period between runs— the standard, proven recovery interval. With gentle increases, as noted in the training programs in this book, your body should rebound stronger than before, ready for a new challenge.

Regularity

To maintain the adaptations, you must regularly exercise every 2-3 days. Waiting longer than this will cause a slight loss in the capacity you have been developing each day. The longer you wait, beyond 3 days, the harder it will be to start up again. Staying regular with your exercise is the best policy.

"Muscle memory"

This is the process by which your neuro-muscular system remembers the patterns of muscle activity which you have done regularly over an extended period of time. The longer you have been walking and running regularly, the more easily it will be to start up when you've had a layoff. During your first month of running, for example, if you miss 3 days of running, it will take a week to get back to the same level, and feel the same way. But, if you have run regularly for 6 months, and you can't run for three days, you won't notice hardly any interruption in your running.

Tip: Cramped for time? Just do 5 minutes

The main reason that beginners don't make progress is that they don't run regularly. Whatever it takes to keep you getting out there, even for 10 minutes, three days a week—do it! Yes, even as little as 5 minutes will maintain some of the adaptations. If you do 5 minutes, you will do 10 on most days, and that will maintain most of the adaptations.

Difference between aerobic and anaerobic exercise

Aerobic means in the presence of oxygen. If you are running aerobically, you will be running slow enough to be within your current capabilities, so that your muscles can get enough oxygen to process the energy in the cells (burning fat in most cases). The minimal waste products produced during aerobic running can be easily removed.

Anaerobic running means going at a pace that is too fast or too long for you, putting you outside of your trained range. Your muscles can't get enough oxygen to burn the most efficient fuel, fat, so they shift to the stored sugar, glycogen. The waste products from this fuel pile up quickly in the cells, tightening the muscles, and causing you to breathe heavily. If you keep running anaerobically, you will have to slow down significantly or stop. Anaerobic running requires a lot longer recovery period.

Fast-twitch or slow-twitch

Why are some people able to run fast, and others slow and steady for the duration? Several decades ago the mystery was solved through research on muscle fibers: those with more fast-twitch fibers can pick up speed quickly for a short distance. Those with an abundance of slow-twitch fibers won't run fast, but can keep running and walking for long distances. Since you are born with one or the other, you may thank your birth parents for the type you have.

Fast twitch fibers are capable of explosive action followed by exhaustion, which can get us into trouble. Once these muscles get in shape, it is easy to go faster at the beginning of a run than you should—without feeling that it is too fast. Most fast twitchers can't understand why they "ran out of gas" at the end of a run because the pace felt so easy at the beginning. The preferred fuel for fast fibers is glycogen (stored sugar). It burns quickly, produces a significant amount of waste, and then is fatigued.

The good news for those with the fast fibers is that longer long runs can adapt these to work as slow twichers. As you extend the length of your long runs, the muscle fibers are recruited, and transformed to burn fat. The most difficult part of long distance training for a fast twitcher is the slowing down of the pace from the beginning of a run. But, once the pace is controlled (and the ego), fast runners find that they don't get exhausted at the end, and significantly push back the endurance limit.

Slow-twitch fibers burn fat naturally, and are, therefore, designed for aerobic endurance exercise. But, unlike fast-twitch fibers, the fat burners cannot be trained to fire quickly to allow for fast running. So, slow twitchers shouldn't count on winning a race by sprinting at the finish.

YOUR JOURNAL WILL INSPIRE YOU

"In a few seconds of writing in your journal,
you control the process of running improvement."

It would be wonderful if we never had to write anything down. In this magic world, you could rely upon your brain to track and retain everything you do, and sort it constantly to prepare you for the next few activities. Then, moments before you were scheduled to do something, a brain transmission would arrive, telling you exactly what to do, where to do it, the materials you need, and the deadline. And, while we're dreaming, this would be done with complete consistency, hour after hour, day after day.

Since we don't operate in a perfect world, with a perfect brain, a journal allows us to plan the future, track our behaviors, learn from our mistakes, and chart our progress in a consistent direction. With a simple logbook format that each of us chooses, we can see what to do, usually within a few minutes, and make the adjustments necessary. Journals give us control over our future while they allow us to learn from our past.

I'm not suggesting that everything be scheduled in advance. Some of the most inspiring moments, and memorable actions sneak up on us unexpected. In your journal, you can trap these, and relive the positive feelings. But, by using your journal to plan ahead, you're programming the brain to continuously steer towards interesting opportunities that arise, as you fine-tune the training and the goal. You don't even have to have a time goal to benefit from a journal. Journals are extremely helpful in ensuring that you schedule and record the enjoyable components while avoiding the stressful trends that produce injury.

Of all the activities that surround running, it is the writing and review of your journal that gives the greatest control over the direction of your running, so that you can make adjustments. It only takes a few minutes every other day to record the key information. Looking back through your entries will provide laughs and enjoyment.

You'll revisit the interesting things you saw during the last week, the crazy thoughts, the people you met, and the fun. This process can inspire the right brain to produce more entertainment, as you schedule runs that promote its activity. You'll read more about this in the motivation chapter.

Journal keepers are more likely to be lifelong runners

Many beginning runners tell me that the writing of each day's mileage in the journal was their greatest motivation—simple but satisfying. After a few weeks, many runners learn the empowerment of organizing their runs in their journal according to their schedule.

By the time 6 months have passed, you'll discover the satisfaction of looking ahead several months to schedule races, the training needed for them, and ensuring that there are fun events along the way. I hear from several runners every month who use their journal as a diary, noting other significant activities, the kid's soccer scores, and PTA notes.

Whatever format you choose, you'll find that by scheduling that very important time to yourself, the run time in the journal, that you actually run more times per week. The journal becomes the steering wheel that keeps you on the road of positive progress. As you hold tight and use the wheel, you feel an empowering sense of making progress.

Restoring order

One runner told me, "When my wife died, my life seemed to be in chaos. I felt a simple and powerful sense of security in documenting the distance that I covered each day. No one could take that away from me." Another runner commented, "As a young executive and a young Mom, I felt that I had no control over my life until I started using a training journal. It started with writing distance, then temperature, pace and route. My journal writing time was the only part of my day when I felt I had control. It was wonderful!"

A simple reward can pull you out of the dumps

We all feel better and enjoy our activities when we feel rewarded. The simple act of recording the distance you cover each day will give you a genuine sense of accomplishment that is felt internally. When you string together a series of runs on days you didn't feel like running, you feel so good inside. Even the most upbeat people have periods of low motivation, and have told me that their journals got them re-focused on the down days.

This is your book

Yes, you are writing a book. At the most basic, you will have an outline of your running life during the next few months. No one tells you what goes into this book. As runners record their entries in the log, they realize that they can use the same journal to organize other areas of life. Even runners who are not fired up about the process at first, are usually impressed at how many benefits flow from this tool. Since you don't need to show anyone your journal, you can let your feelings go as you write. Upon review, your emotional response to a given workout can be very interesting months or years later.

Can you capture the fleeting thoughts of the right brain?

One of the interesting challenges, and great rewards of journaling is noting the creative, and sometimes crazy images that emerge from the right side of our head. On some days, you won't get any of these, and on others...the faucet opens up. Often the thoughts come out of nowhere. Other times, you will be suddenly hit with a solution to a problem you've been working on for months. If you have your journal available at the place where you return from your run, for example your car, office desk, kitchen countertop, you can quickly jot some key words to describe the images or craziness.

The various types of journals

Calendar—facing you on the wall

Many runners start recording their runs on a wall calendar, or one that is posted on the refrigerator. Looking at the miles recorded is empowering. But, equally motivating for many is seeing too many "zeros" on days that should have been running days. If you're not sure whether you will really get into this journal process, you may find it easiest to start with a calendar.

An organized running journal

When you use a product that is designed for running, you don't have to think to record the facts. The spaces on the page ask you for certain info, and you will learn to fill it very quickly.

This leaves you time to use some of the open space for the creative thoughts and ideas that pop out during a run. Look at the various journals available, and pick one that looks to be easier to use, and to carry with you.

Notebook

You don't need to have a commercial product. You can create your own journal by using a basic school notebook of your choice. Find one of the size that works best with your lifestyle (briefcase, purse, etc.). Below you will find the items that I've found helpful for most runners to record.

But, the best journals are those that make it easier for you to collect the data you find interesting, while allowing for creativity. The non-limiting nature of a notebook is a more comfortable format for runners that like to write a lot one day, and not so much another day.

Computer logs

There are a growing number of software products that allow you to sort through information more quickly. In working with a company (PC Coach) to incorporate my training program, I discovered that this format speeds up the search for information you need. As you set up your own codes and sections, you can pick data that is important to you, sort it to see trends, and plan ahead. Some software (including mine) allows for you to download data from a heart monitor or GPS watch.

The writing process

1. Capturing the flow from the right brain

Try to have the log handy, so that you can record info after a run. Immediately after a run, you will have fresh perceptions, and will be more likely to record the right brain images and thoughts that tend to fade quickly.

2. Just the facts

At first, spend a few seconds, and quickly jot down the key info that you want recorded. If you have to think about an item, skip it and just fill in the items you can fill in quickly. Here are a list of items that many runners use:

Date:
Morning Pulse
Time of run:
Distance covered:
Time running:
Weather:
Temp
Precipitation
Humidity

> *Comments:*
> Walk-Run frequency
> Any special segments of the run (speed, hills, race, etc.)
> Running companion
> Terrain
> How did you feel (1-10)

Go back over the list again, and fill in more details—emotional responses, changes in energy or blood sugar level, and location of places where you had aches and pains—even if they went away during the run. You are looking for patterns of items that could indicate injury, blood sugar problems, lingering fatigue, etc.

3. Helpful additions (usually in a blank section at the bottom of the page)

- Improvement Thoughts
- Things I should have done differently
- Interesting Happenings
- Funny things
- Strange things
- Stories, right brain crazy thoughts

Are you tired…or just lazy? Your morning pulse may tell

Many people say that they are too tired to run. But, after interviewing many who make this claim, I've come to believe that most of the reasons for this sensation is laziness (most will admit this), or low blood sugar. One of the best indicators of real fatigue is your resting pulse, taken in the morning. Your journal can track this (although some runners use a piece of graph paper).

Recording morning pulse

1. As soon as you are conscious—but before you have thought much about anything—count your pulse rate for a minute. Record it before you forget it. If you don't have your journal by your bed, then keep a piece of paper handy with a pen.

2. It is natural for there to be some fluctuations based upon the time you wake up, how long you have been awake, etc. But, after several weeks and months, these will balance themselves out. The ideal would be to catch the pulse at the instant that you are awake, before the shock of an alarm clock, thoughts of work stress, etc.

3. After 2 weeks or so of readings, you can establish a base line morning pulse. Take out the top 2 high readings, and then average the readings.

4. The average is your guide. If the rate is 5% higher than your average, take an easy day. When the rate is 10% higher, and there is no reason for this (you woke up from an exciting dream, medication, infection, etc.), then your muscles may be tired indeed. Take the day off if you have a walk-run scheduled for that day.

5. If your pulse stays high for more than a week, call your doctor to see if there is a reason for this (medication, hormones, metabolic changes, etc.).

WHY DOES YOUR BODY WANT TO HOLD ONTO FAT?

Fat is our biological insurance policy against disaster. It is the fuel your body can use, in case of starvation, sickness, injury to the digestive system, etc. You'll read a bit later about how the "set point" inside you programs your body to hold onto fat, too well. I've spent years looking into this topic, and talking to experts in the field. This chapter will explain my beliefs about the process, so that you can set up a strategy based upon your needs and goals.

Many people start running to burn fat. Indeed, the run-walk method is probably the most effective and convenient exercise mode for re-organizing your fat storage to burn fat because it helps you enjoy endurance exercise—which becomes your fat-burning furnace. When the body is conditioned for fat burning, it prefers this as fuel because of the small amount of waste product produced.

But, it's not enough to burn the fat. For long term health and body management, you need to keep it off. Successful fat burners do three things:

1. Understand the process by reading this chapter and other sources,
2. Truly believe that they can lower the body fat percentage,
3. Set up a behavioral plan that works into their lifestyles.

How does fat accumulate?

When you eat some fat during a snack or a meal, you might as well put it into a syringe, and inject it into your stomach or thigh. A gram of fat eaten is a gram of fat processed, and put into the fat storage areas on your body. In addition, when you eat more calories than you need during a day from protein (fish, chicken, beef, tofu) and carbohydrate (breads, fruits, vegetables, sugar), the excess is converted into fat and stored.

Fat for survival

More than a million years of evolution have programmed your body to hold on to the fat you have stored because of a simple principle: the survival of the species. Before humans understood disease and prevention, they were susceptible to sweeping infections. Even mild diseases and flu wiped out a significant percentage of the population each year in primitive times. Those who had adequate fat stores survived periods of starvation and sickness, and passed on the fat accumulation adaptation to their children.

The powerful set point holds onto our fat

The set point is a biologically engineered survival mechanism. While it does seem possible to adjust it, you are going into battle against mechanisms that have been in place for over a million years. By understanding it, however, you can do some of the many little things that have been effective in fat management.

Fat level is set in early 20s

Many experts agree that by about the age of 25 we have accumulated a level of fat that the body intuitively marks as it's lowest level. The set point is programmed to increase a little each year. Let's say that John had 10% body fat at age 25, and his set point increased by half a percent per year. The amount of increase is so small when we are young that we usually don't realize that we're adding it—until about 10 years later when it's time to go to a class reunion or something.

We humans are supposed to carry around fat. But, your set point does too good a job continuing to add to the percentage, each year, every year. And, the amount of increase seems to be significantly greater as we get older. Even when you've had a year when stress or illness prevented the usual increase, the set point makes up by increasing appetite during the following year or two. Go ahead, shout "Unfair!" as loud as you wish. Your set point doesn't argue, it just sets you up for another deposit. Exercise can lower the set point…so hold onto your hope.

Men and women deposit fat differently

While men tend to deposit fat on the surface of the skin, women (particularly in their 20s and 30s) fill up internal storage areas first. Most women will acknowledge that their weight is rising slightly, year by year, but aren't concerned because there is no noticeable fat increase on the surface. Some judge this by the "pinch test."

Then, during one year, the internal storage areas fill up, and the extra fat starts accumulating on the stomach, thighs and other areas. A common woman's complaint in the 30s or early 40's is the following. "My body has betrayed me." In fact, fat has been deposited at a fairly consistent rate but hidden from view for many years.

Men find it easier to burn fat than women

When men start running regularly, many lose fat and weight for several months. Probably related to biological issues, and primitive protections for mothers, women have a harder time losing fat. The reality is that you are ahead of the others in our society even if you are maintaining the same weight. Because of the set point, one would expect an average 45 year old person in the US to gain 3-4 pounds a year. So, the set point may be lowering even if you are holding at the same weight, year to year.

Diets don't work because of the "starvation reflex"

We are certainly capable of lowering food intake for days, weeks and months to lower fat levels and weight. This is a form of starvation and the set point has a long-term memory. So, we lose that 10 pounds during the 2 months before the class reunion. Then, when you stop the diet, you will experience a starvation reflex: a slight increase in appetite and hunger, over weeks and months until the fat accumulated on your body is higher that it was before the diet. It's a fact that almost all of those who lose fat on a diet put more pounds back on the body within months of going off the diet.

Waiting too long to eat triggers the starvation reflex

When you wait more than 3 hours without eating something, your set point organism senses that you may be going into a period of starvation. The longer you wait to eat, the more you will feel these three effects of the starvation reflex:

1. There is a reduction in your metabolism rate. Imagine an internal voice saying something like this, "If this person is going to start depriving me of food, I had better tune down the metabolism rate to conserve resources." A slower metabolism makes you feel more lethargic, drowsy, and unmotivated to exercise or move around. In fact, you tend to stay in your chair or on the couch, minimizing motion and calorie burning.

2. There is an increase in the fat-depositing enzymes. The longer you wait to eat something, the more enzymes you will have, and the more fat will be actually deposited from your next meal.

3. Your appetite will increase. The longer you wait to eat, the more likely it is that, for the next few meals, you will have an insatiable appetite. You eat a normal meal, and you're still hungry.

Suddenly depriving yourself of decadent foods

I used to like a particular type of ice cream so much that I ate a quart or more of it, several nights a week. It was the reward I gave myself for reaching my exercise goals for that day. Then, on a fateful New Year's day, my wife Barb and I decided to eliminate the chocolate chip mint ice cream from our diet—after more than 10 years of enjoyment. We were successful for 2 years. A leftover box after a birthday party got us re-started on the habit, and we even increased our intake over what it had been before—due to having deprived ourselves.

You can "starve" yourself of a food that you dearly love for an extended period of time. But, at some time in the future, when the food is around and no one else is.....you will over-consume that food. My correction for this problem was the following:

1. I made a contract with myself: I could have a little of it whenever I wanted while promising to be "reasonable."
2. I set a goal to enjoy one bowl a week 5 years from now.
3. Four years from now, I'll enjoy a bowl every 5 days.
4. Three years from now, I'll enjoy a bowl every 4 days.
5. I will learn to enjoy healthy, sweet things, like fruit salads, energy bars, etc.

It worked! I hardly ever eat any ice cream...but sometimes enjoy a bowl if I want. This is purely for medicinal reasons you understand.

The low-carbohydrate scam

There is no doubt that low carb diets can help you lose weight....water weight. Such a loss is superficial and easily gained back. Here's how it works. To perform physical exertion, you need a quick energy source called glycogen, which comes from eating carbohydrates, and must be replenished every day. The storage areas for glycogen are limited, and glycogen is also the primary source for vital organs like the brain. A good quantity of water is stored near the glycogen storage areas because it is needed when glycocen is processed.

By starving themselves of carbohydrates, low carb dieters experience a severe reduction in glycogen. But, if the glycogen isn't there, water is not stored either. The elimination of these two substances can produce a significant weight loss within days—continuing for a few weeks.

Fat is not being burned off. In fact, fat storage is encouraged in many of the low carb diets. As low carb dieters eat more fat, they often increase the fat while the water/glycogen loss will show as weight loss due to the superficial loss of water. When they replace the water and glycogen later, the weight goes back on. Soon, the overall body weight is greater than before because of the extra fat from the low carb diet.

Because the glycogen energy source is low or depleted, low carbers will not have the energy for exercise. This is why you will hear folks on this diet complain of low energy, lack of desire to exercise, inability to finish a workout, and sometimes mental lack of focus (low glycogen means less fuel for the brain).

Even if you "tough it out", or cheat on the diet a little, your capacity to do even moderately strenuous exertions will be greatly reduced. With your energy stores near empty, exercising becomes a real struggle, and no fun.

Low carb diets don't tell you this....

- You don't burn fat—many gain fat.
- The weight loss is usually water loss with glycogen loss.
- Almost everyone on this diet resumes regular eating within a few weeks or months.
- Almost all low carb dieters gain back more weight than they lost.
- You lose the energy and motivation to exercise.
- You lose exercise capacity that can help to keep the weight off when you resume eating normally.
- Your metabolism rate goes down making it harder to keep the weight off.

This is a type of starvation diet. I've heard from countless low carb victims who admit that while they were on the diet, their psychological deprivation of carbs produced a significant rebound effect when they began eating them again. The cravings for bread, pastries, french fries, soft drinks, and other pound-adding foods increased for months after they went off the diet. The weight goes back on, and on, and on.

Like so many diets, the low-carb diet reduces the metabolism rate. This reduces the number of calories you burn per day just living. When you return to eating a regular diet, you will not have a "metabolism furnace" to burn up the increased calories.

Lowering the set point

Your body has a wonderful ability to adapt to the regular activities that you do. It also tries to avoid stress. In the next chapter, we will talk about how to condition your muscles to be fat burning furnaces. Once you get them into shape to do this, you can move into a fat burning lifestyle. Lowering the set point is more complex, but possible when you are regularly putting certain types of stress on your system.

Endurance running: a positive stress on the body which can stimulate adaptations in two areas

- body temperature increase.
- pounding or bouncing.

Running regularly, long enough to produce these stresses, will trigger a search for ways of reducing the stress.

- Increases core body temperature.

Everyone knows that when you run, you get warm or hot. The work required to lift your body off the ground raises your core body temperature. If you sustain this increase, it puts a heat stress on the system. Since body fat acts like a blanket in maintaining body temperature, the body's intuitive, long term solution is to reduce the size of the fat blanket around you, which then reduces the heat buildup.

The more regular you are with run-walks that build up to more than 45 minutes, the more likely it is that your set point will be reduced to avoid this repeated stress. It also helps even more to have one run-walk every week that goes beyond 90 minutes.

- Bouncing and pounding.

The more weight you carry, the more you will feel the pounding effect of running. If you run as often as every other day, your body senses this regular stress, and searches for ways of reducing it. It will tend to recognize that the reduction of the extra fat baggage will reduce the bouncing stress.

Cross training for fat burning

To maintain a regular dose of set-point lowering stress, while minimizing orthopedic stress, cross training can help. The best activities are those that raise core body temperature, use a lot of muscle cells, and can be continued comfortably for more than 45 minutes. Cross training is done on days when you don't run. Swimming is not a good fat-burning exercise. The water absorbs temperature buildup, and therefore core body temperature doesn't rise significantly.

Good fat burning exercises
- Nordic track
- Walking
- Elliptical
- Rowing
- Exercise cycle

WHY SOME PEOPLE BURN A LOT MORE FAT

Even if you don't lose a pound, if you run regularly, you'll receive a series of health benefits. Studies at the Cooper Clinic, founded by Dr. Kenneth Cooper in Dallas, TX. and other organizations, have shown that even obese people lower their risk factors for heart disease when they exercise regularly.

Slow, aerobic running is one of the very best ways to burn fat. But most runners, during their first year, usually hold their own showing no weight loss. This is actually a victory over the set point. First, you are avoiding the average set point inspired increase of 3-4 pounds a year. But, runners are actually burning fat by maintaining weight. How can this be? Read on.

As you run, your body stores more glycogen and water all over the body to process energy, and cool you off. Your blood volume also increases. All of these internal changes help you exercise better, but they cause a weight gain (not a fat gain). If your weight is the same a year after starting regular exercise, you have burned off several pounds of fat. Don't let the scales drive you crazy.

Long term fat burnoff usually requires some discipline and focus. If you will take responsibility for managing your eating and doing your running and walking, you will succeed. One secret to fat burning success is being more active all day long. Once you learn to walk instead of sit, you will be amazed at how many steps you will take per day:

Steps = Calories Burned

Aerobic running burns fat

When you are taking liberal walk breaks, and running totally within your physical capacity (no huffing and puffing), your muscles are being supplied with enough oxygen to do the work. They are aerobic. If you run too hard, you overwhelm the capacity of the muscles, the blood system cannot deliver enough oxygen to the muscles and you are anaerobic.

Oxygen is needed to burn fat. Therefore, running at an easy pace will keep you in the aerobic, or "fat burning" zone. When you run too fast, for that day, and your muscles can't get enough oxygen you will huff and puff. This is the sign that you are building up an oxygen debt. Without oxygen, the muscles turn to stored glycogen, which produces a high amount of waste product.

Fat burning training program

- One long run-walk a week of 60 min +
- Two run-walks of 45 min +
- 2-3 alternative exercise sessions of 45 min +
- Taking an additional 6000 (or more) steps a day in your daily activities

Sugar-burning during the first 15 min. of exercise

Glycogen is the quick access fuel your body uses during the first quarter hour of exercise. Those who don't exercise longer than 15 minutes will not get into fat burning, and won't train their muscles to burn this fuel. But, if you have been depriving yourself of carbohydrates, as when on a low-carb diet, you'll have trouble with energy and motivation.

Glycogen produces a high amount of waste product—mostly lactic acid. If you move slowly with mostly walking, there is no significant buildup. Even when the pace feels slow, if you are huffing and puffing within the first 10 minutes, you have been going too fast. When in doubt, extend your walking at the beginning and go slower.

From 15 minutes to 45 minutes you will transition into fat burning

If you are exercising within your capabilities, your body starts to break down body fat, and use it as fuel. Fat is actually a more efficient fuel, producing less waste product. This transition continues for the next 30 minutes or so. By the time you've been exercising within your capabilities for 45-50 minutes, you will be burning mostly fat if the muscles are trained to do this. With lots of walking, and a slow pace, almost anyone can work up to three sessions of 45 minutes each.

Three sessions a week in the fat burn zone

Even the most un-trained muscles that have only burned glycogen for 50 years can be trained to burn fat under one condition:

- Get into the fat-burning zone 3 times a week (45 + min. a week).

One session a week beyond 90 minutes

The endurance session is designed to keep you in the fat burning zone for an extended period. For best results, this should be done every week, and should increase gradually to around 90 minutes. If you don't have time for a 90 minute session, shoot for 60 minutes.

"By running and walking for 90 minutes each week, the leg muscles become fat burners. Over time, this means that you will burn more fat when you are sitting around all day at your desk, and even burn it when you are sleeping at night."

Walk breaks allow you to go farther without getting tired

This pushes you into the fat burning zone while allowing for a quick recovery of the muscles. For fat-burning purposes, it is best to walk earlier, and walk more often. The number of calories you burn is based upon the number of miles covered. Walk breaks allow you to cover more distance each day without tiring yourself.

By lowering the exertion level, you will stay in the fat burning zone longer—usually for the whole session. When in doubt, it's best to walk more and slow down.

FAT BURNING TRAINING: FOR THE REST OF YOUR LIFE

Earlier in this book there is a very successful fat burning training program. Once you have reached the end of this schedule, I have designed the following for continuing to do what you have started—and move to a higher level if you wish. The following is ideal, but many runners don't have the time to do every component. I have assigned priorities next to each item.

(1) Top priority workouts—be sure to do these each week.

(2) Second priority workouts—it would be very beneficial to do these each week.

(3) Do these if you have time they will help; just have a lower priority.

Days of the week are listed only as a suggestion. Feel free to adjust to your schedule. If you cannot do the total length of the session, do whatever you can—even 10 minutes is better than nothing. Walking is a great way to burn extra calories on a running or non running day. Using a step counter will allow you to break up the walking into an all day series of step segments. See the section below on 10,000 steps a day.

Sunday (1)

One longer walk-run. Start with the amount that you finished up with at the end of your fat burning program (usually 60 minutes), and gradually increase to between 90 and 120 minutes. Once you reach the time that you want as your limit, you can adjust the run-walk ratio as you feel comfortable. Don't be afraid to put more walking in the beginning. The mission here is to keep going while feeling good. You should finish knowing that you could have run farther.

Monday (3)

An alternative exercise that raises body temperature while allowing you to continue for 60 + minutes. Even on time-crunched days, try to shoot for 45 minutes. Even if you can only squeeze in 15 minutes, the extra calories burned will help in total fat burning for the week. Stair machine work is not recommended.

Tuesday (1)
A moderate walk-run of 40-60 minutes. These allow you to maintain the fat-burning adaptations gained in the longer one on the weekend. These could be done at whatever pace you wish, but when in doubt—go slower—and go longer.

Wednesday (3)
Alternative exercise, same as Monday 60 minutes.

Thursday (1)
Same as Tuesday 40-60 minutes.

Friday (3)
Alternative exercise, same as Monday 60 minutes.

Saturday (3)
You can have this day off if you wish. Because it is the day before your long one, it's best to take it very easy if you do any exercise. A short and gentle walk would be fine, for example, but you need fresh muscles for the long one.

How much walking and how much running?
Follow the guidelines in the Galloway Run-Walk Method chapter, and "Setting Yourself Up For Running Success." In the beginning, you will be running a few seconds and walking for 1-2 minutes. Very gradually you will increase the amount of running. Don't push too quickly. It would be better to choose a ratio that seems too easy for you.

10,000 more steps a day on non running days/6000 on running days
A pedometer, or step counter, can change your life. They give you an incentive and a reinforcement for adding extra

steps to your day. It also gives you a sense of control over your actual calorie burnoff. Once you get into the goal of taking more than 10,000 steps a day in your everyday activities, you find yourself getting out of your chair more often, parking farther away from the supermarket, walking around the kid's playground, etc.

These devices are usually about one inch square, and clip onto your belt, pocket, or waistband. The inexpensive models just count steps, and this is all you need. Other models compute miles and calories.

I recommend getting one from a quality manufacturer. When tested, some of the really inexpensive ones registered 3-4 times as many steps as the quality products did—walking exactly the same course.

Your goal is to accumulate an additional 10,000 steps at home, at work, going shopping, waiting for kids, etc. on your non-running days, and 6000 on your running days. This is very doable. You will find many pockets of time during the day when you are just sitting or standing. When you use these to add steps to your day, you burn fat and feel better. You become a very active person.

About dinnertime you should do a "step check." If you haven't acquired your 10,000 (or 6000), walk around the block a few extra times after dinner. You don't have to stop with these figures. As you get into it, you'll find many more opportunities to walk....and burn.

15-30 pounds of fat....gone

Depending upon how many times you do the following each week, you have some opportunities each day to burn a little here, and a little there. These are easy movements that don't produce tiredness, aches or pains, but at the end of the year—it really adds up:

Lbs. per year	Activity
1-2 pounds—	taking the stairs instead of the elevator
1-2 pounds—	getting out of your chair at work to walk down the hall
1-2 pounds—	getting off the couch to move around the house (but not to get potato chips)
1-2 pounds—	parking farther away from the supermarket, mall, etc.
1-3 pounds—	parking farther away from your work
2-4 pounds—	walking around the kids playground, practice field (chasing the kids)
2-4 pounds—	walking up and down the concourse as you wait for your next flight
3-9 pounds—	walking the dog each day
2-4 pounds—	walking a couple of times around the block after supper
2-4 pounds—	walking a couple of times around the block during lunch hour at work
2-4 pounds—	walking an extra loop around the mall, supermarket,etc. to look for bargains (this last one could be expensive when at the mall)

Total: 18-40 pounds a year

15 more pounds burned each year from adding a few extra miles a day

By using time periods when you usually have small pockets of time, you can add to your fat-burning without feeling extra fatigue:

- Slow down and go one more mile on each run.
- Walk a mile at lunchtime.
- Jog a mile before dinner, or afterward.

FAT BURNING: THE INCOME SIDE OF THE EQUATION

Gaining control over your calorie intake is crucial for body fat reduction. Runners often complain that even though they have increased mileage, and faithfully done their cross training workouts, they are not losing weight. In every case, when I have questioned them, each did not have a handle on the amount of calories they were eating. In every case, when they went through the drill of quantifying, each was eating more than they thought. Below you will find ways to cut 10 or more pounds out of your diet without starving yourself.

Websites tell you calorie balance and nutrient balance

The best tool I've found for managing your food intake is a good website or software program. There are a number of these that will help to balance your calorie balance sheet (calories burned vs calories eaten).

Most of these will have you log in your exercise for the day, and what you eat. At the end of the day, you can retrieve an accounting of calories, and of nutrients. If you are low on certain vitamins or minerals, protein, etc., after dinner, you can eat food or take a vitamin pill. Some programs will tell vegetarians whether they have received enough complete protein since this nutrient is harder to put together from vegetable sources. If you haven't received enough of some nutrient, you can do something about it that night, or the next morning to make up the deficit. If you ate too many calories, walk after dinner or boost tomorrow's workouts, or reduce the calories, or both.

I don't recommend letting any website control your nutritional life until the end of your days. At first, it helps to use it every day for 1-2 weeks. During this time, you'll see patterns, and note where you tend to need supplementation or should cut back. Every week or two, do a spot check during 2-3 days. Some folks need more spot checks than others. If you are more motivated to eat the right foods and quantities by logging in every day, go for it.

For a list of the websites, see my website: **www.jeffgalloway.com**. Try several out before you decide.

A portion of most foods is about the size of a fist

Portion Control—through logging your food intake

Whether you use a website or not, a very productive drill is that of logging what you eat every day for a week. Bring a little note pad, and a small scale if you need it. As people log in, and then analyze the calories in each portion, they are almost always surprised at the number of calories they are eating. The fat content is often another surprise. Many foods have the fat so well disguised that you don't realize how much you are eating.

After doing this drill for several days, you start to adjust the amount that you eat each meal. You are gaining control! Many runners have told me that they resented the first week of logging in, but it became fairly routine after that. Once you get used to doing this, you become aware of what you will be putting in your mouth, and are taking charge over your eating behaviors.

Eating every 2 hours

As mentioned in the previous chapter, if you have not eaten for about 3 hours, your body senses that it is going into a starvation mode, and slows down the metabolism rate while increasing the production of fat-depositing enzymes.

This means that you will not be burning as many calories as is normal, that you won't be as mentally and physically alert, and that more of your next meal will be stored away as fat.

If the starvation reflex starts working after 3 hours, then you can beat it by eating every 2 hours. This is a great way to burn more calories. A person who now eats 2-3 times a day, can burn 8-10 pounds a year when they shift to eating 8-10 times a day. This assumes that the same calories are eaten every day, in the same foods.

Big meals slow you down

Big meals are a big production for the digestive system. Blood is diverted to the long and winding intestine and the stomach. Because of the workload, the body tends to shut down blood flow to other areas, leaving you feeling more lethargic and sedentary.

Small meals speed you up

Smaller amounts of food can usually be processed quickly without putting a burden on the digestive system. Each time you eat a small meal or snack, your metabolism speeds up. Faster metabolism, several times a day is calories burned.

You also give a setback to your set point

When you wait more than three hours between meals the set point engages the starvation reflex. But if you eat every

2-3 hours, the set point is not engaged due to the regular supply of food. Therefore, the fat depositing enzymes don't have to be stimulated.

Motivation increases when you eat more often

The most common reason I've found for low motivation in the afternoon is not eating regularly enough during the day—especially during the afternoon. If you have not eaten for 4 hours or more, and you're scheduled for a run that afternoon, you will not feel very motivated because of low blood sugar and low metabolism. Even when you have had a bad eating day, and feel down in the dumps, you can gear up for a run-walk by having a snack 30-60 minutes before exercise. A fibrous energy bar with a cup of coffee (tea, diet drink) can reverse the negative mindset. But, you don't have to get yourself into this situation if you eat every 2-3 hours.

Satisfaction from a small meal—to avoid overeating

The number of calories you eat per day can be reduced by choosing foods and combinations of foods that leave you satisfied longer. Sugar is the worst problem in calorie control and satisfaction. When you drink a beverage with sugar in it, the sugar will be processed very quickly, and you will often be hungry within 30 minutes—even after consuming a high quantity of calories. This will usually lead to two undesirable outcomes:

1. Eating more food to satisfy hunger.

2. Staying hungry and triggering the starvation reflex.

Your mission is to find the right combination of foods in your small meals that will leave you satisfied for 2-3 hours. Then, eat another snack that will do the same. You will find a growing number of food combinations that probably have fewer calories, but keep you from getting hungry until your next snack.

Nutrients that leave you satisfied longer:

Fat

Fat will leave you satisfied from a small meal because it slows down digestion, but a little goes a long way. When the fat content of a meal goes beyond 30%, you start to feel more lethargic due to the fact that fat is harder to digest. While up to about 18% of the calories in fat will help you hold hunger at bay, a lot of fat can compromise a fat-burning program. Fat is automatically deposited on your body. None of it is used for energy. When you eat a fatty meal, you might as well inject it onto your hips or stomach. The fat you burn as fuel must be broken down from the stored fat on your body. So, it helps to eat a little fat, but a lot of it will mean more fat on your body.

There are two kinds of fat that have been found to cause narrowing of the arteries around the heart and leading to your brain: saturated fat and trans fat. Mono and unsaturated fats, from vegetable sources, are often healthy: olive oil, nuts, avocado, safflower oil. Some fish oils have Omega 3 fatty acids which have been shown to have a protective effect on the heart. Many fish have oil that is not protective.

Look carefully at the labels because a lot of foods have vegetable oils that have been processed into trans fat. A wide range of baked goods and other foods have trans fat. It helps to check the labels, and call the 800 number for foods that don't break down the fat composition—or avoid the food.

Protein—lean protein is best.

This nutrient is needed, every day, for rebuilding the muscle that is broken down continuously, as well as normal wear and tear. Runners, even those who log high mileage, don't need to eat significantly more protein than sedentary people.

But, if runners don't get their usual amount of protein, they feel more aches and pains, and general weakness sooner than average people.

Having protein with each meal will make you feel satisfied for a longer period of time. But eating too many protein calories than you need will produce a conversion of the excess into fat.

Recently, protein has been added to sports drinks with great success. When a drink with 80% carbohydrate and 20% protein (such as Accelerade) is consumed within 30 minutes of the start of a run, glycogen is activated better, and energy is supplied sooner and better.

By consuming a drink that has the same ratio(like Endurox R4) within 30 minutes of the finishing of a run, the reloading of the muscles has been shown to be more complete.

Complex carbohydrates give you a "discount" and a "grace period.

Foods such as celery, beans, cabbage, spinich, turnip greens, grape nuts, whole grain cereal, etc., can burn up to 25 % of the calories in digestion. As opposed to fat (which is directly deposited on your body after eating it) it is only the excess carbs that are processed into fat. After dinner, for example, you have the opportunity to burn off any excess that you acquired during the day.

Fat + Protein + Complex Carbs = SATISFACTION
Eating a snack that has a variety of the three satisfaction ingredients above will lengthen the time that you'll feel satisfied—even after some very small meals. These three items take longer to digest, and therefore, keep the metabolism rate revved up.

Other important nutrients...

Fiber

When fiber is put into foods, it slows down digestion and maintains the feeling of satisfaction longer. Soluable fiber, such as oat bran, seems to bestow a longer feeling of satisfaction than unsoluable fiber such as wheat bran. But, any type of fiber will help in this regard.

Recommended percentages of the three nutrients

There are differing opinions on this issue. Here are the ranges given by a number of top nutritionists that I have read and asked. These are listed in terms of the percentage per day of each of the calories consumed in each nutrient, compared to the total number of calories per day.

Protein:	between 20% and 30%
Fat:	between 15% and 25%
Carbohydrate:	whatever is left—hopefully in complex carbohydrates.

Simple carbs help us put weight back on the body

We're going to eat some simple carbohydrates. These are the "feel good" foods: candy, baked sweets, starches like mashed potatoes and rice, sugar drinks (including fruit juice and sports drinks) and most desserts. When you are on a fat burning mission, you need to minimize the amount of these foods.

The sugar in these products is digested so quickly that you get little or no lasting satisfaction from them. They often leave you with a craving for more of them, which, if denied, will produce a starvation reflex. Because they are processed quickly, you become hungry relatively quickly and will eat, accumulating extra calories that usually end up as fat at the end of the day.

As mentioned in the last chapter, it is never a good idea to cut them out and say "I'll never eat another." This sets up a starvation reflex time bomb ticking. Keep taking a bite or two of the foods you dearly love, while cultivating the taste of foods with more fiber, and little or no refined sugar or starch.

GOOD BLOOD SUGAR = MOTIVATION

The blood sugar level (BSL) determines how good you feel. When it is at a good, moderate, regular level you feel good, stable and motivated. If you eat too much sugar, your BSL can rise too high. You'll feel really good for a while, but the excess sugar triggers a release of insulin that usually pushes it too low. In this state, you don't have energy, mental focus is foggy, and motivation goes down rapidly.

When blood sugar level is maintained throughout the day, you will be more motivated to exercise, and feel like adding other movement to your life. You'll have a more positive mental attitude, and be more likely to deal with stress and solve problems. Just as eating throughout the day keeps metabolism up, the steady infusion of balanced nutrients all day long will maintain stable blood sugar levels.

You don't want to get on the "bad side" of your BSL. Low levels are a stress on the system, and literally mess with your mind. Your brain is fed by blood sugar and when the supply goes down, your mental stress goes up.

If you have not eaten for several hours before a run-walk, you'll receive an increase in the number of negative messages telling you you don't have the energy to exercise, that it will hurt, and many others.

The simple act of eating a snack that has carbohydrate and about 20% protein will reduce the negative messages, make you feel good, and get you out the door. Keeping a snack as a BSL booster can often be the difference whether you get out and run that day, or not.

The BSL roller coaster

Eating a snack with too many calories of simple carbohydrate can be counter-productive for BSL maintenance. As mentioned above, when the sugar level gets too high, your body produces insulin, sending BSL lower than before. The tendency is to eat again, which produces excess calories that are converted into fat. But if you don't eat, you'll stay hungry and pretty miserable—in no mood to exercise or move around and burn calories, or get in your run for the day.

Eating every 2-3 hours is best

Once you find which snacks work best to maintain your BSL, most people maintain a stable blood sugar level better by eating small meals regularly, every 2-3 hours. As noted in the previous chapter, it's best to combine complex carbs with protein, and a small amount of fat.

Do I have to eat before running?

Only if your blood sugar is low. Most who run-walk in the morning don't need to eat anything before the start. As mentioned above, if your blood sugar level is low in the afternoon, and you have a run scheduled, a snack can help

when taken about 30 minutes before the run. If you feel that a morning snack will help, the only issue is to avoid consuming so much that you get an upset stomach.

For best results in raising blood sugar when it is too low (within 30 minutes before a run) a snack should have about 80% of the calories in simple carbohydrate and 20% in protein. This promotes the production of insulin which is helpful before a run in getting the glycogen in your muscles ready for use. The product Accelerade has worked best among the thousands of runners I hear from every year. It has the 80%/20% ratio of carb to protein. If you eat an energy bar with the 80/20 ratio, be sure to drink 6-8 oz of water with it.

Eating during exercise

Most exercisers don't need to worry about eating or drinking during a run-walk until the length of the session exceeds 90 minutes. At this point, there are several options. In each case, wait until you have been exercising for 40 minutes before starting.

GU or Gel products—these come in small packets, and are the consistency of honey or thick syrup. The most successful way to take them is to put 1-2 packets in a small plastic bottle with a pop-top. About every 10-15 minutes, take a small amount with a sip or two of water.

Energy Bars—cut into 8-10 pieces and take a piece, with a couple of sips of water, every 10-15 minutes.

Candy—particularly gummi bears or hard candies are good. The usual consumption is 1-2 about every 10 minutes

Sports Drinks—since there is a significant percentage of nausea among those who drink during exercise, this is not my top recommendation. If you have found this to work for you, use it exactly as you have used it before.

It is important to re-load after exercise— within 30 minutes

Whenever you have finished a hard or long workout (for you), a reloading snack will help you recover faster. Again, the 80/20 ratio of carb to protein has been most successful in reloading the muscles. The product that has worked best among the thousands I work with each year is Endurox R4.

AN EXERCISER'S DIET

A radical change in the foods you eat, is not a good idea, and usually leads to problems. In this chapter, I will explain the items that are most important, and can help in maintaining good overall health and fitness.

As a regular exerciser you will not need significantly more vitamins and minerals, protein, etc. than a sedentary person. But if you don't get these ingredients for several days in a row, you will feel the effects when you try to exercise.

Most important nutrient: water

Whether you take in your fluids with water, juice or other fluids, drink regularly throughout the day. Under normal circumstances, your thirst is a good guide for fluid consumption. I will not tell you that you must drink 8 glasses of water a day because I've not seen any research to back this up. Fluid researchers who follow this topic tell me that the research says that if we drink regularly and when thirsty, fluid levels are replaced fairly quickly.

If you are having to take bathroom stops during walks or runs, you are usually drinking too much—either before or during the exercise.

During an exercise session of 60 minutes or less, most exercisers don't need to drink at all. The intake of fluid before exercise should be arranged, so that the excess fluid is eliminated before the run. Each person is a bit different, so you will have to find a routine that works for you.

Even during extremely long runs of over 4 hours, medical experts from major marathons recommend no more than 27 oz. an hour of fluid. Most folks need much less than this.

Sweat the electrolytes

Electrolytes are the salts that your body loses when you sweat: sodium, potassium, magnesium and calcium. When these minerals get too low, your fluid transfer system doesn't work as well, and you may experience ineffective cooling, swelling of the hands, and other problems.

Most runners have no problem replacing these in a normal diet, but if you are experiencing cramping during or after exercise, regularly, you may be low in sodium or potassium. The best product I've found for replacing these minerals is called SUCCEED. If you have high blood pressure, get your doctor's guidance before taking any salt supplement.

Practical eating issues

- You don't need to eat before a run, unless your blood sugar is low. (See the previous chapter.)
- Reload most effectively by eating within 30 min. of the finish of a run (80% carb/20/protein).
- Eating or drinking too much right before the start of a run will interfere with deep breathing, and may cause side pain. The food or fluid in your stomach limits your intake of air into the lower lungs, and restricts the diaphram.
- If you are running low on blood sugar at the end of your long runs, take some blood sugar booster with you. (See the previous chapter for suggestions.)
- It is never a good idea to eat a huge meal. Those who claim that they must "carbo load" are rationalizing the desire to eat a lot of food. Eating a big meal the night before (or the day of) a long run can be a real problem. You will have a lot of food in your gut, and you will be bouncing up and down for an extended period. Get the picture?

When you are sweating a lot, it is a good idea to drink several glasses a day of a good electrolyte beverage. Accelerade, by Pacific Health Labs, is the best I've seen for both maintaining fluid levels and electrolyte levels.

Run-Walk eating schedule

- 1 Hour before a morning run: either a cup of coffee or a glass of water
- 30 min. before any run (if blood sugar is low) @100 calories of Acclerade
- Within 30 min. after a run: @200 calories of a 80% carb/20% protein snack (Endurox R4, for example)
- If you are sweating a lot during hot weather, 3-4 glasses of a good electrolyte beverage like Accelerade

Meal ideas

Breakfast options

1. Whole grain bread made into french toast with fruit yogurt, juice, or frozen juice concentrate as syrup
2. Whole grain pancakes with fruit and yogurt
3. A bowl of Grape Nuts Cereal, skim milk, non fat yogurt, and fruit

Lunch options

1. Tuna fish sandwich, whole grain bread, a little low fat mayo, cole slaw (with fat free dressing)
2. Turkey breast sandwich with salad, low fat cheese, celery & carrots
3. Veggie burger on whole grain bread, low fat mayo, salad of choice
4. Spinach salad with peanuts, sunflower seeds, almonds, low fat cheese, non fat dressing, whole grain rolls or croutons

Dinner options

There are lots of great recipes in publications such as **COOKING LIGHT**. The basics are listed below. What makes the meal come alive are the seasonings which are listed in the recipes. You can use a variety of fat substitutes.

1. Fish or lean chicken breast or tofu (or other protein source) with whole wheat pasta, and steamed vegetables
2. Rice with vegetables, and a protein source
3. Dinner salad with lots of different vegetables, nuts, lean cheese or turkey, or fish, or chicken

I recommend Nancy Clark's books. Her *Sports Nutrition Guidebook* is a classic.

RUNNING FORM

When you understand the nature of running, you can better understand the most efficient way of running. I believe that running is an inertia activity: your mission is just to keep the momentum. Very little strength is needed to run. The first few strides get you into motion, and your focus is to stay in motion. To reduce fatigue, aches and pains, your body intuitively fine-tunes your motion, so that you minimize effort as you continue to run about every other day, month after month.

Humans have many bio-mechanical adaptations working for them, which have been made more efficient over more than a million years of walking and running. The anatomical origin of efficiency in humans is the combination of the ankle and the Achilles tendon.

This is an extremely sophisticated system of levers, springs, balancing devices, and more—involving hundreds of component parts amazingly well coordinated. Bio-mechanics experts believe that this degree of development was not needed for walking. When our ancient ancestors had to run to survive, the evolution reached a new level of performance.

When we have the right balance of walking and running, a very little amount of effort from the calf muscle produces a smooth continuation of forward movement. As the calf muscle gets in better shape, and improves endurance, you can keep going for mile after mile with little perceived effort. Other muscle groups offer support and fine-tune the process. When you feel aches and pains that might be due to the way you run, going back to the minimal use of the ankle and achilles tendon can often leave you feeling smooth and efficient very quickly.

A better way of running?

There may be a better way to run for you; one that will leave your legs with more strength and fewer aches and pains. The fact is, however, that most runners are not far from great efficiency. Repeated research on runners has shown that most are running very close to their ideal. I believe this is due to the action of the right brain. After tens of thousands of steps, it keeps searching for (and then refines) the most efficient pattern of feet, legs, and body alignment. In my running schools and weekend retreats, I conduct an individual running form analysis with each runner. After having analyzed over 10 thousand runners, I've also found that most are running in a very efficient way. The problems are seldom big ones—but a series of small mistakes. By making a few minor adjustments, most runners can feel better on every run.

The big three: posture, stride, and bounce

In these consultations, I've also discovered that when runners have problems, they tend to occur in three areas: Posture, stride, and bounce. And the problems tend to be very individual occurring most often in specific areas because of specific motions. Fatigue brings on most of the problems relating to form. Slight over stride, for example creates fatigue, and then weakness at the end of a run. As a tired body "wobbles", other muscle groups try to keep the body on course, but are not designed for this.

Three negative results of inefficient form:

1. Fatigue becomes so severe that it takes much longer to recover.
2. Muscles are pushed so far beyond their limits that they break down and become injured.
3. The experience is so negative that the desire to run is reduced, producing burnout.

Almost everyone has some slight problem. I don't suggest that everyone should try to create perfect form. But when you become aware of your form problems, and make changes to keep them from producing aches and pains, you'll feel fewer aches, smoother running, and experience faster times. This chapter can help you understand why aches and pains tend to come out of form problems—and how you may be able to reduce or eliminate them.

Your own form check

In some of my clinics, I use a digital camera that gives instant feedback. If you have one of these cameras, have a friend take pictures of you running from the side (not running towards or away from the camera) while you run on a flat surface. Some runners can check themselves while running alongside stores that offer a reflection in a plate glass window. The sections below will tell you what to look for.

If you feel relaxed and running is easy even at the end of a run—you're probably running correctly

Overall, the running motion should feel easy. There should be no tension in your neck, back, shoulders or legs. A good way to correct problems is to change posture, foot or leg placement, etc., so that running is easier and there is no tightness or pain.

Posture

Good running posture is actually good body posture. The head is naturally balanced over the shoulders, which are aligned over the hips. As the foot comes underneath, all of these elements are in balance, so that no energy is needed to prop up the body. You shouldn't have to work to pull a wayward body back from a wobble or inefficient motion.

Forward lean

The posture errors tend to be mostly due to a forward lean—especially when we are tired. The head wants to get to the finish as soon as possible, but the legs can't go any faster. In their first races, beginners are often the ones whose heads are literally ahead of the body, which produces more than a few falls around the finish line. A forward lean will often concentrate fatigue, soreness, and tightness in the lower back, or neck.

It all starts with the head. When the neck muscles are relaxed, the head is usually in a natural position. If there is tension in the neck, or soreness afterward, the head is usually leaning too far forward. This triggers a more general upper body imbalance in which the head and chest are suspended slightly ahead of the hips and feet. Ask a running companion to tell you if and when your head is too far forward, or leaning down. The ideal position of the head is mostly upright with your eyes focused about 30-40 yards ahead of you.

Sitting back

The hips are the other major postural area where runners can get out of alignment. A runner with this problem, when observed from the side, will have the butt behind the rest of the body. When the pelvis area is shifted back, the legs are not allowed to go through a natural range of motion, and the stride length becomes short. This produces a slower pace, even when spending significant effort. Many runners tend to hit harder on their heels when their hips are shifted back.

A backward lean is rare

It is rare for runners to lean back, but it happens. In my experience, this is usually due to a structural problem in the spine or hips. If you do this, and you're having pain in the neck, back or hips, you should see a doctor.

Correction: "Puppet on a string"

The best correction I've found to postural problems has been this mental exercise: imagine that you are a puppet on a string. Suspended from up above like a puppet—from the head and each side of the shoulders—your head lines up above the shoulders, the hips come directly underneath, and the feet naturally touch lightly. It won't hurt anyone to do the "puppet" several times during a run.

It helps to combine this image with a deep breath. About every 4-5 minutes as you start to run after a walk break, take a deep, lower lung breath, straighten up and say "I'm a puppet." Then, imagine that you don't have to spend energy maintaining this upright posture because the strings attached from above keep you on track. As you continue to do this, you reinforce good posture, and work on making this behavior a habit.

Upright posture not only allows you to stay relaxed; you will probably improve your stride length. When you lean forward, you'll be cutting your stride to stay balanced. When you straighten up, you'll receive a stride bonus of an inch or so without any increase in energy.

An oxygen dividend
Breathing improves when you straighten up. A leaning body can't get ideal use out of the lower lungs. This can cause side pain. When you run upright, the lower lungs can receive adequate air, absorb the oxygen better, and reduce the chance of side pain.

Feet low to the ground
The most efficient stride is a shuffle—with feet right next to the ground. As long as you pick your foot up enough to avoid stumbling over a rock or uneven pavement, stay low to the ground. Most runners don't need to get more than 1" clearance.

Your ankle combined with your Achilles tendon will act as a spring, moving you forward on each running step. If you

stay low to the ground, very little effort is required. Through this "shuffling" technique, running becomes almost automatic. When runners err on bounce, they try to push off too hard. This usually results in extra effort spent in lifting the body off the ground. You can think of this as energy wasted in the air; energy that could be used to run another mile or two.

The other negative force that penalizes a higher bounce is that of gravity. The higher you rise, the harder you will fall. Each additional bounce off the ground delivers a lot more impact on feet and legs—which on long runs produces aches, pains and injuries.

The correction for too much bounce: Light touch

The ideal foot placement should be so light that you don't usually feel yourself pushing off or landing. This means that your foot stays low to the ground, and goes through an efficient and natural motion. Instead of trying to overcome gravity, you get in synch with it.

Here's a "light touch drill": during the middle of a run, time yourself for 20 seconds. Focus on one item; touching so softly that you don't hear your feet. Earplugs are not allowed for this drill. Imagine that you are running on thin ice, or through a bed of hot coals. Do several of these 20 second touches, becoming quieter and quieter. You should feel very little impact on your feet as you do this drill.

Stride length

Studies have shown that as runners get faster, the stride length shortens. This clearly shows that the key to faster and more efficient running is increased cadence or turnover of feet and legs.

A major cause of aches, pains and injuries is a stride length that is too long. At the end of this chapter, you'll see a list of problems and how to correct them. When in doubt, it is always better to err on the side of having a shorter stride.

Don't lift your knees!

Even world class distance runners don't do this because it tires the quadracep muscle (front of the thigh), leading to a stride that is too long to be efficient. The most common time when runners stride too long is at the end of a tiring run. This slight overstride, when the legs are tired, will leave your quads (front of thigh) sore the next day or two.

Don't kick out too far in front of you!

If you watch the natural movement of the leg, it will kick forward slightly as the foot gently moves forward in the running motion to contact the ground. Let this be a natural motion that produces no tightness in the muscles behind the lower or upper leg.

Tightness in the front of the shin, or behind the knee, or in the hamstring (back of the thigh) is a sign that you are kicking too far forward, and reaching out. Correct this by staying low to the ground, shortening the stride, and lightly touching the ground.

Cadence or turnover drill

This is an easy drill that improves the efficiency of running, making running easier. This drill excels in how it helps to pull all the elements of good running form together at the same time. Over the weeks and months, if you do this drill once every week, you will find that your normal cadence slowly increases naturally.

1. Warm up by walking for 5 minutes, and running and walking very gently for 10 minutes.
2. Start jogging slowly for 1-2 minutes, and time yourself for 30 seconds. During this half minute, count the number of times your left foot touches.
3. Walk around for a minute or so.
4. On the second 30 second drill, increase the count by 1 or 2.
5. Repeat this 3-7 more times. Each time trying to increase by 1-2 additional counts.

In the process of improving turnover, the body's internal monitoring system coordinates a series of adaptations which pulls together all of the form components into an efficient team:

- Your foot touches more gently.
- Extra, inefficient motions of the foot and leg are reduced or eliminated.
- There is less effort is spent on pushing up or pushing forward.
- You stay lower to the ground.
- The ankle becomes more efficient.
- Ache and pain areas are not overused.

Walking form

Walking form is usually not an issue when walking at a gentle, strolling pace. But every year, there are runners who get injured because they are walking in a way that aggravates some area of the foot or leg. Most of these problems come from trying to walk too fast, with too long a stride, or from using a race-walking or power-walking technique.

1. *Avoid a long walking stride.* Maintain a relaxed motion that does not stress the knees, tendons or muscles of the leg, feet, knees or hips. If you feel pain or aggravation in these areas, shorten your stride. Many runners find that they can learn to walk fairly fast with a short stride. But when in doubt, use the walk for recovery and ease off.

2. *Don't lead with your arms.* Minimal arm swing is best. Swinging the arms too much can encourage a longer walk stride which can push into aches and pains quickly. The extra rotation produced can also aggravate hips, shoulder, and neck areas. You want the legs to set the rhythm for your walk and your run. When this happens, you are more likely to get into the "zone" of the right brain.

3. *Let your feet move the way that is natural for them.* When walkers try techniques that supposedly increase stride length by landing further back on the heel, or pushing further on the toe (than the legs are designed to move), many get injured.

RUNNING INJURY FREE

Because running is a primitive survival activity, we have all of the capabilities and potential adaptations to run without injury or pain. When we have a correct balance of stress and rest, with gentle increases, we can continue to improve, and enjoy our runs. The single greatest reason for improvement in running is *not getting injured.*

But, inside each human is a personality trait that can compromise running enjoyment. I call this the "Type A overworker syndrome." Even those who feel they have no competitive urges and no athletic background need to be on guard. Once a new runner has achieved a certain level of fitness, there is a tendency to push more or rest less. At first, the body responds. When the runner keeps pushing, the body breaks at one of the "weak links."

Be sensitive to weak links

Each of us has a very few areas that take on more stress, and tend to get most of the aches, pains and injuries. The most common areas are the knees, the foot, the shins, and the hip. Those who have been running for a year or more will usually know their own weak links. If you have a particular place on your knee that has been hurt before, and it hurts after a run, take an extra day or two off, and follow the suggestions on treating an injury listed below.

How do you know that you are injured?

The following are the leading signs that you have an injury. If you feel any of the three below, you should stop your workout immediately, and take some extra rest days (usually 2-3). Running (and sometimes even walking) at the early stages of an injury creates a dramatically worse injury—even on one run. If you take 2-3 days off at the first symptom, you may avoid having to stop exercise for 2-3 months when running on the injury. It is always safer to err on the side of taking more time off.

1. Inflammation—any type of swelling

2. Loss of function—the foot, etc., doesn't work correctly

3. Pain—that does not go away when you walk for a few minutes

Losing conditioning

Studies have shown that you can maintain conditioning even when you don't exercise for 5 days. Surely you want to continue regular running, but staying injury free has an even higher priority. So, don't be afraid to take up to 5 days off when a "weak link" kicks in. In most cases, you will only stop for 2-3 days.

Treatment

It is always best, at the first sign of injury, to see a doctor (or with muscle injury a massage therapist) who wants to get you out there running as soon as possible.

The better doctors will explain what they believe is wrong (or tell you when he/she cannot come up with a diagnosis) and give you a treatment plan. This will give you great confidence in the process, which has been shown to speed the healing.

Treatments while you are waiting to see a doctor

Unfortunately, most of the better doctors are so booked up that it takes a while to see them. While waiting for your appointment, here are some things other runners have done with success when one of the weak links shows inflammation, loss of function or pain:

1. Take at least 2-5 days off from any activity that could irritate it.
2. If the area is next to the skin (tendon, foot, etc.), rub a chunk of ice on the area(s)—constantly rubbing for 15 minutes until the area gets numb. Continue to do this for a week after you feel no symptoms.
3. If the problem is inside a joint or muscle, call your doctor and ask if you can use prescription strength anti-inflammatory medication. Don't take any medication without a doctor's advice—and follow that advice.
4. If you have a muscle injury, see a very successful sports massage therapist. Try to find one who has a lot of successful experience treating the area where you are injured. The magic fingers and hands can often work wonders.

Preventing injury

Having had over a hundred injuries myself, and then having worked with tens of thousands who have worked through aches and pains, I've developed the suggestions below. They are based upon my experience in advising as one runner to another. I'm proud to report that since I started following the advice that I give others, I've not had an overuse injury in over 25 years.

Take 48 hours between runs

Running puts a lot more stress on the muscles than walking. Allowing the running muscles to rest for two days will provide a magic time period for recovery. Stair machine work should also be avoided during the 48 hour rest period (stair work uses the same muscles as running). Also avoid any other activities that seem to irritate the tendon.

Don't stretch!

I've come full circle on this. A high percentage of the runners who report to me, injured, have either become injured because they stretched or aggravated the injury by stretching. When they stop stretching, a significant percentage report that the injury heals enough to run in a relatively short period of time.

The exception to this rule is when you have Ilio-tibial band injury. For this injury alone, stretching the I-T band seems to help runners continue to run while they heal.

Do the "toe squincher" exercise

This exercise can be done 10-30 times a day on both feet (one at a time). Point the toes and squinch them until the foot cramps (only a few seconds). This strengthens the many little muscles in the foot that can provide a platform of support. It is particularly effective in preventing plantar fascia.

Don't increase total mileage more than 10% a week

Monitor your mileage that you run (walking is usually OK) in a log book or calendar. If you exceed the 10 per cent increase on a given week, take an extra day off.

Drop total mileage in half, every 3rd or 4th week

This is helpful even when increasing by no more than 10% per week

Your log book can guide you here also. You won't lose any conditioning and you'll help the body heal itself, and get stronger. A steady increase, week after week, does not allow the legs to catch up and rebuild.

Avoid a long stride—both walking and running

Running with more of a shuffle (feet close to the ground) reduces the chance of many injuries. Even walking with a long stride can irritate the shin muscles. Read the "Running Form" section for more information on developing an efficient running form.

YOUR FIRST RACE

I know, you aren't competitive. You have no need to race. That's fine. But the neighborhood road races that you see all over the country are primarily for motivation. The participants in the average road race are folks like yourself that are trying hard to stay motivated. Enrolling in a race is a commitment to yourself to do the training each week to prepare.

Most runners who arrive at their first race are surprised to see that most of the participants are average looking people. Sure, there are always a few lean folks on the front line who are going for the trophy. Everyone else is there to share the excitement of the event, and to celebrate the moment of finishing.

Races are fun. If the energy could be put in a container, and used in your car, you wouldn't have to buy gasoline for your car for weeks. Once you have attended a race, you will want to go back. This is one place where almost everyone is in a good mood.

What to look for in a race

- Fun and Festive—held in an interesting area, part of a town festival, music, or expo with exhibits.
- Well organized—the organizers...keep things organized: no long lines, easy to register, start goes off on time, water on the course, refreshments for all—even the slowest, no major problems.
- Refreshments—some races have water, others have a buffet.
- A good T-shirt or other reward—you'll wear it with pride.
- The organizers focus on average or beginning runners.

Where to find out about races

Running stores

This resource is at the top of our list because you can usually get entry forms plus some editorial comment about the race. Explain to the store folks that this is your first race, and you want to enjoy the whole experience. Select a fun event that has a high rating in the "what to look for" section, just above.

Friends who run

Call a friend who has run for several years. Tell him or her that you are looking for a fun, upbeat race about every month. Go over the same categories listed above. Be sure to ask the friend for a contact number or website where you can find more information on the event, and possibly enter. As with running store folks, the editorial comments and evaluation of an event can steer you to a good experience.

Running clubs

If there is a running club or two in your area, get in touch. The officers or members can steer you in the direction of events. Running clubs may be found by doing a web search:

type "running clubs (your town)." The RRCA (Road Runner's Club of America) is a national organization of neighborhood clubs. From their website, search for a club in your area.

Newspaper listings

In many newspapers, there is a listing of community sports events in the weekend section. This comes out on Friday or Saturday in most cities, usually in the lifestyle section. Some listings can be in the sports section under "running" or "road races." You can often find these listings on the website of the newspaper.

Web searches

Just do a web search for "road races (your town)" or "5K (your town)." There are several event companies that serve as a registration center for many races: including **www.signmeup.com www.active.com** From these sites you can sometimes find an event in your area, research it, and then sign up.

How to register

1. Online. More and more of the road running events are conducting registration online. This allows you to bypass the process of finding an entry form, and sending it in before the deadline.
2. Fill out an entry and send it in. You will need to fill out your name, address, T-shirt size, etc., and then sign the waiver form. Be sure to include a check for the entry fee.
3. Show up on race day. Because some races don't do race day registration, be sure that you can do this. There is usually a penalty for waiting until the last minute—but you can see what the weather is like before you make the trek to the race.

Most common race distance is a 5K (3.1 miles)

This is an excellent choice for your first race because it's about the shortest distance usually run, and in most areas you will have many from which to choose. Choose a race far enough in the future, so that you can build up a long run-walk. Stage your training, so that you finish a training run-walk that is 1-2 miles longer than the distance you plan to run in the race about 7-10 days before the race itself.

The long run is your training program for your race

You will notice from your schedule that you have one longer run-walk each week on the weekend. At first, this is run entirely by time.

Once your weekend run-walk has reached 30 minutes, you should run one of these on the track every month for 2 or 3 months, so that you can compute the distance you ran. Each lap around a standard track is about .25 mile. A 5K is actually 12.5 laps.

While some runners like to do their long runs around a track, others become very bored when they run there. Running 1-2 laps at the beginning, in the middle, and at the end of the run will allow you to get a handle on how fast you are running, so that you can compute your distance for the day when running off the track.

Each week add about .25 to .4 miles to the distance of the long run. You want to run slower on the long runs than on your shorter weekly run-walks. Take the walk breaks as you need to avoid huffing and puffing. It is the distance covered that builds endurance, go slower

Here is a schedule of long runs to prepare for a 5K after you have reached 30 minutes as your long run:

WEEK #	Long Run Distance
1.	2.25 miles
2.	2.5 miles
3.	2.75 miles
4.	3.0 miles
5.	3.25 miles
6.	3.5 miles
7.	3.75 miles
8.	4.0 miles
9.	4.25 miles
10.	4.5 miles
11.	5K Race

Rehearsal

If at all possible, run one or more of your long runs on the race course. You'll learn how to get there, where to park (or which rapid transit station to exit), and what the site is like. If you will be driving, drive into the parking area several times to make sure you understand how to go exactly where you need to park. This will help you to feel at home with the staging area on race day. Run over the last half mile of the course at least twice. This is the most important part of the course to know. It's also beneficial to do the first part of the course to see which is best for walk breaks (sidewalks, etc.)

Visualize your line up position: at the back, along the side of the road. If you line up too far forward, you could slow down runners that are faster. You want to do this first race slowly, and have a good experience. This is most likely at the back of the pack. Because you will be taking your walk breaks, as in training, you need to stay at the side of the road. If there is a sidewalk, you can use this for your walk breaks.

Food—eat what you have eaten before your harder runs. It is OK not to eat at all before a 5K unless you are a diabetic, then go with the plan that you and your doctor have worked out.

Get your bearings—walk around the site to find where you want to line up (at the back of the pack), and how you will get to the start. Choose a side of the road that has more shoulder or sidewalk for ease in taking walk breaks.

Register or pick up your race number—if you already have all of your materials, you can bypass this step. If not, look at the signage in the registration area, and get in the right line. Usually there is one for "race day registration" and one for those who registered online, or in the mail and need to pick up their numbers.

Start your warm up 40-50 minutes before the start. If possible, go backwards on the course for about .5-.6 miles and turn around. This will give you a preview of the most important part of your race—the finish. Here is the warmup routine:

- Walk for 5 minutes, slowly.
- Walk at a normal walking pace for 3-5 minutes, with a relaxed and short stride.
- Start your watch for the ratio of running and walking that you are using, and do this for 10 minutes.
- Walk around for 5-10 minutes.
- If you have time, walk around the staging area, read your jokes, laugh, relax.
- Get in position and pick one side of the road or the other where you want to line up.
- When the road is closed, and runners are called onto the road, go to the curb and stay at the side of the road, near or at the back of the crowd.

After the start

Remember that you can control how you feel during and afterward by conservative pacing and walks.

- Stick with your run/walk ratio that has worked for you; take every walk break, especially the first one.
- If it is warm, slow down and walk more.
- Don't let yourself be pulled out too fast on the running portions.
- As people pass you, who don't take walk breaks, tell yourself that you will catch them later—you will.
- If anyone interprets your walking as weakness, say: "This is my proven strategy for a strong finish."
- Talk with folks along the way, enjoy the course, smile often.
- On warm days, pour water over your head at the water stops (no need to drink on a 5K unless you want to).

At the finish

- In the upright position
- With a smile on your face
- Wanting to do it again

After the finish

- Keep walking for at least half a mile.
- Drink about 4-8 oz. of fluid.
- Within 30 min. of the finish, have a snack that is 80% carbohydrate/20% protein (Endurox R4 is best).
- If you can soak your legs in cool water during the first two hours after the race, do so.
- Walk for 20-30 minutes later in the day.

The next day

- Walk for 30-60 minutes, very easy. This can be done at one time, or in installments.
- Keep drinking about 4-6 oz. an hour of water or sports drink like Accelerade.
- Wait at least a week before you either schedule your next race or vow to never run another one again.

ACHES & PAINS

Many people will try to tell you that running will hurt your joints. According to the research, they are wrong. I've seen the reports in medical journals, and heard the summaries from various top orthopedists. According to these reports that span several decades, runners have healthier joints than those who did not exercise.

While most running aches are preventable, almost everyone who starts a running program makes a mistake or two. But almost all of the aches that come from training mistakes, go away with a couple of days of rest from exercise.

After about 50 years of running, I've had just about every injury runners can have. I'm proud to say, as I write this book, that for more than a quarter century, I have not had a single overuse injury. It's not that hard to stay injury free. The methods that I have used I pass on to you as one runner to another in this chapter.

For medical advice, see a doctor who wants to get you running and walking

The content in this chapter is not medical advice. At the first sign of a medical problem, see a doctor. I suggest that you find one who has treated a lot of runners, and wants to get you back out there, walking and running. The same resources as are mentioned in choosing a race are the ones to tap in looking for a doctor: running stores, running clubs, friends who have run for a few years, and websites. The American Medical Athletic Association, which is combined with the American Running Association, has a referral list of sports medicine doctors used by many runners.

Weak links

Everyone has certain areas of the body that tend to take more abuse when you exercise. The common areas for runners are knees, feet, hips and shins. But you may have other areas based upon the unique way that you run and walk. After you have had a few aches, you will get to know the weak links. Be very sensitive to each of them.

Don't push through pain

Pushing on where there is significant aches or pains can increase the damage by multiples. At the first sign of pain, I will walk. After a minute or two, I will jog for a few seconds and walk again. After 3 or 4 of these repetitions, if the pain is still there, I will stop the run. In fact, I haven't had to stop a run for more than 10 years. If you take 1-2 days off at the beginning stage of an injury, you can avoid taking weeks or months off later. It is always better to err on the side of rest if there is even a slight chance that you may be injured.

Top 3 situations that produce running injuries

"It hurts but I only have one more mile...I'll finish the run."

"It may hurt a little, but I don't think it's anything."

"It's so nice today; I can't do much damage by running on my injury."

Signs that it may be an injury

- Swelling: there is inflammation in an area that is affected by running.

- Loss of function: the foot, knee, etc doesn't work as it usually does.

- Pain! If the pain doesn't go away when you have taken several minutes of rest or slow walking.

The "Don'ts" Of injury treatment

1. Don't stretch—except for Ilio-tibial band injury.
2. Don't use heat.
3. Don't do any activity for 2 days that could aggravate the area.

Quick treatment tips

For all injuries

1. Take 3 days off from running or any activity that could aggravate the area.
2. Avoid any activity that could aggravate the injury.
3. As you return to running, stay below the threshold of further irritation.

Muscle injuries

1. Call your doctor's office, and see if you can take prescription strength anti inflammatory medication.
2. See a sports massage therapist who has worked successfully on many runners.

Tendon and foot injuries

1. Rub a chunk of ice directly on the area for 15 minutes every night (keep rubbing until the area gets numb—about 15 minutes).

    Note: ice bags, or gel ice don't seem to do any good at all

2. Foot injuries sometimes are helped by an air cast.

Knee injuries

1. Call your doctor's office to see if you can take prescription strength anti-inflammatory medication.
2. Gentle walking sometimes helps.
3. Sometimes the knee straps can relieve pain; ask your doctor.

Shin injuries

1. If the pain gradually goes away as you walk on it, there is less worry of a stress fracture.
2. But if the pain hurts more as you walk or run on it—see a doctor! (possible stress fracture)

Starting back running before the injury has healed

With most running injuries, you can continue to run even while the injury is healing. But first, you must have some time off to get the healing started. If you do this at the beginning of an injury, you will usually only need 2-5 days off. The longer you try to push through the problem, the more damage you produce, and the longer it will take to heal. Stay in touch with the doctor at any stage of this healing/running process, and use your best judgement.

To allow for healing, once you have returned to running, stay below the threshold of further irritation. In other words, if the injury feels a little irritated when running at 2.5 miles, and starts hurting a little at 3 miles, you should run no more than 2 miles. And if your run-walk ratio is 30 sec run/1 min walk, you should drop back to 15 seconds run and 90 seconds walk.

Always allow a day of rest between running days. With most injuries you can cross train to maintain conditioning, but make sure that your injury will allow this. Again, your doctor can usually advise on this.

Best cross training modes to maintain your running conditioning

Before doing any of these ask your doctor. Most are fine for most injuries. But, some run a risk of irritating the injured area and delaying the healing process. For more information on this, see the chapter on cross training in my *Galloway's Book On Running* (second edition).

Gradually build up the cross training because you have to condition those muscles gradually also. Even walking is a great way to maintain conditioning if the injury and the doctor will allow it.

1. Running in the water can improve your running form.
2. Nordic Track machines
3. Walking
4. Rowing machines
5. Eliptical machines

There is much more information on specific injuries in my *Galloway's Book On Running* (second edition). But here are some helpful items that I want to pass on as one runner to another.

KNEE PAIN

Most knee problems will go away if you take 5 days off. Ask your doctor if you can use anti-inflammatory medication. Try to figure out what caused the knee problem. Look at the most worn pair of shoes you have, even walking shoes. If there is wear on the inside of the forefoot, you probably overpronate. If you have repeat issues with knee pain, you may need a foot support or orthotic. If there is pain under the kneecap, or arthritis, the glucosamine/chondroitin products have helped. The best I've found in this category is Joint Maintenance Product by Cooper Complete.

OUTSIDE OF THE KNEE PAIN—Iliotibial Band Syndrome

This band of fascia acts as a tendon going down the outside of the leg from the hip to just below the knee. The pain is most commonly felt on the outside of the knee, but can be felt anywhere along the I-T band. I believe this to be a "wobble injury." When the running muscles get tired, they don't keep you on a straight running track. The I-T band tries to restrain the wobbling motion, but it cannot and gets overused. Most of the feedback I receive from runners and doctors is that once the healing has started (usually a few days off from running), most runners will heal as fast when you run on it as from a complete layoff. It is crucial to stay below the threshold of further irritation.

Treatment for Ilio-tibial Band:

1. Stretching: Stretch before, after, and even during a run. Here are several stretches that have worked for this injury.
2. Massage: a good massage therapist can tell whether massage will help and where to massage. The two areas for possible attention are the connecting points of the connective tissue that is tight, and the fascia band itself in several places.
3. Walking is usually fine, and a tiny bit of running is usually OK.
4. Direct ice massage on the area of pain: 15 minutes of continuous rubbing every night.

SHIN PAIN—"Shin Splints" or Stress Fracture

Almost always, pain in this area indicates a minor irritation called "shin splints" that allows running and walking as you heal. The greatest pain or irritation during injury is during the start of a run or walk, which gradually lessens or goes away as you run and walk. It takes a while to fully heal, so you must have patience.

Irritation of the inside of the leg, coming up from the ankle is called "posterior tibial shin splints" and is often due to over pronation of the foot (foot rolls in at pushoff). When the pain is in the muscle on the front of the lower leg, it is "anterior tibial shin splints. This is very often due to having too long a stride when running, and especially when walking. Downhill terrain should be avoided as much as possible during the healing.

If the pain is in a very specific place, and increases as you run, it could be a more serious problem: a stress fracture. This is unusual for beginning runners, but characteristic of those who do too much, too soon. It can also indicate low bone density. If you even suspect a stress fracture, do not run or do anything stressful on the leg, and see a doctor. Stress fractures take weeks of no running and walking, usually wearing a cast. They may also indicate a calcium deficiency.

HEEL PAIN—Plantar Fascia

"The most effective treatment is putting your foot in a supportive shoe before your 1st step in the morning."

This very common injury hurts when you first walk on the foot in the morning. As you get warmed up, it gradually goes away, only to return the next morning. The most important treatment is to put your foot in a supportive shoe before you step out of bed each morning. Be sure to get a "shoe check" at a technical running store to make sure that you have the right shoe for your foot. If the pain is felt during the day, and is painful, you should consult with a podiatrist. Usually the doctor will construct a foot support that will surround your arch and heel. This does not need to be a hard orthotic, but usually a softer one designed for your foot with build-ups in the right places. The "toe squincher" exercise noted in this book can help provide foot strength that will also support the foot. It takes several weeks for this to take effect. This is another injury that allows for running as you heal, but stay in touch with your doctor.

BACK OF THE FOOT—Achilles Tendon

The Achilles tendon is the narrow band of tendon rising up from the heel and connecting to the calf muscle. It is part of a very efficient mechanical system, acting as a strong rubber band to leverage a lot of work out of the foot, with a little effort from the calf muscle. It is usually injured due to excessive stretching, either through running or through stretching exercises. First, avoid any activity that stretches the tendon in any way. It helps to add a small heel lift to all shoes, which reduces the range of motion. Every night, rub a chunk of ice directly on the tendon. Keep rubbing for about 15 minutes, until the tendon gets numb. Bags of ice or frozen gels don't do any good at all in my opinion. Usually after 3-5 days off from running, the icing takes hold and gets the injury in a healing mode. Anti-inflammatory medication very rarely helps with the Achilles tendon.

HIP AND GROIN PAIN

There are a variety of elements that could be aggravated in the hip area. Since the hips are not prime movers in running, they are usually abused when you continue to push on, after getting very tired. The hips try to do the work of the leg muscles, and are not designed for this. Ask your doctor about prescription strength anti inflammatory medication, as this can often speed up recovery. Avoid stretching, and any activity that aggravates the area.

Yoga and Pilates?

I communicate with runners about every week who get injured because they stretched during these programs. Even mild stretches that are outside your range of motion can be adverse to the joints, and tendons. The philosophical benefits of Yoga can be as significant as those from running. If you benefit from such mental benefits go through the sessions—but don't stretch.

Ilio-tibial Band injury—the only major exception

The ilio-tibial is a band of fascia that acts as a tendon. It starts at the hip and continues along the outside of each leg, attaching in several places below the knee. Besides the stretch noted here, individuals find that there are specific

stretches that will help to release the tightness of their I-T band. Those who suffer from this injury can stretch before, after, or during a run-walk, or whenever it tightens up and/or starts to hurt. There is more on this injury in the injury section of this book.

Don't feel guilty if you don't stretch before you run-walk

A gentle walk for 5 minutes, followed by a very gradual transition from walking to run-walk has been the most effective warm up that I have found.

If you have individual stretches that work.... DO THEM!

I've met several people who have certain stretches that seem to help them. If you find a stretch that works for you, go ahead. Just be careful.

STRENGTHENING

There are a few strengthening activities that can help your running. But I must tell you that overall, I don't believe that running is a strength activity. As noted in the "running form" chapter, running is done most effectively, in my opinion, when you use your momentum. I call running an "inertia activity." In other words, you get your body into motion with a few steps, then just maintain that momentum. Therefore, the strength you need for running is minimal. With these facts on the table, it won't surprise you that this chapter is quite short.

Just look at the physiques of the faster runners. There is hardly any muscle development, and no bulk. Carrying around extra superstructure that doesn't help you move forward is extra work for the body—causing a slowdown later in a long run. In strength contests with other athletes that I have attended, runners tend to score at the bottom. When I competed at the world-class level, I didn't know a single competitor who spent an hour doing weight work, on a regular basis—unless their high school or college track coach made them do it.

Note: these exercises are not meant to be prescriptions for medical problems. They are offered from one runner to another because thousands have reported benefit from them. If you have a back or other medical issue, make sure your doctor and other specialists give you permission to use these exercises.

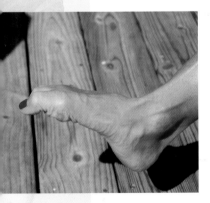

Toe Squincher—for prevention of injuries of the foot and lower leg

I believe that this exercise will help just about every person that runs and walks. Whether barefooted or not, point your toes and contract the muscles of your foot until they cramp. It only takes a few seconds for this to happen. You can repeat this exercise 10-30 times a day, every day.

This is the best way I know to prevent a foot injury called plantar fascia—but it strengthens the areas all over the foot and ankle for better support. I've also heard from runners who believe it has helped to prevent Achilles tendon problems.

Postural muscle exercises

By balancing the strength of muscles on the upper body, that support your posture, you'll tend to maintain positive upright posture while running, walking, or in other of life's activities. In the upright position that is natural for you, running is easier. You'll move forward more efficiently with less energy required for keeping your body balanced.

Good postural muscles will also allow for more efficient breathing. You'll be able to breathe deeply, which will reduce side pain, and enable you to maximize oxygen absorption.

There are two groups of muscles that need to be strengthened. On the front side, the abdominal group provides support and balance. When ab strength is balanced by back and neck muscles, you will resist fatigue in the shoulders, neck, and back.

Front muscles: the crunch

Lie on your back on a cushioned carpet or floor pad with adequate cushioning for your back. Bend your knees. Now raise your head and upper back very slightly off the floor. Go up an inch or two and down, but don't let the upper back hit the floor. As you move very slightly, don't let the stomach muscles relax; keep them working as you go up and down in this very narrow range of motion. It also helps, as you are doing this, to roll slightly to either side, continuously moving. This strengthens the whole range of muscle groups that support the front side of your torso.

For the back, shoulders and neck: arm running

Holding a dumbell in each hand while standing (not while running) go through a range of motion that you would use when running. Keep the weights close to your body as the hands swing from your waist up to your shoulders, and return.

Pick a weight that makes you feel, after a set of 10 repetitions, that you got a workout out of the muscles involved.
But, don't have so much weight that you have to struggle as you get your last 1-2 reps. Start with one set of 10, and increase to 3-5 sets, once or twice a week. This can be done on a running day, or on a rest day.

Prescriptive exercises

These are designed for those who feel that they need more support in one or more of the areas listed below. Those who have had regular aches, pains or injuries in one of the areas below have received benefit from these exercises.

Knees—the stiff leg lift

If you have weak knees, here is an exercise that strengthens the various muscles in the thigh. By developing strength in the range of muscles above, you may tighten the connections around the knee getting better support.

When this group, the quadraceps, have more strength, and you keep your foot in a small range of motion directly below the hips, the knee has less stress.

Sit on a tall bench or table. With a stiff leg, lift the leg up and down, gradually changing the range of motion from inside to outside. Start with no weight, and one set of 10 lifts. When you can easily do 3 sets of 10 lifts with each leg, add a few pounds using a bag or pocketbook, looped around the ankle.

Shins—2 exercises

The foot lift

Sit on a bench with the knee bent at a right angle. Your foot must be significantly off the floor. Hang a bag or pocket book with a pound of weight over the foot. Lift your foot up and down 10 times. Move the angle of the foot to the inside and the outside. Add more weight as a set of 10 feels easy.

Heel walking

Use a very padded shoe. Walk on your heels, so that your toe region is off the floor. Start with 10 steps, and increase until you can do 2-3 sets of 20-30 steps.

STAYING MOTIVATED

- Consistency is the most important part of conditioning and fitness.
- Motivation is the most important factor in being consistent.
- You can gain control over your motivation—every day.

The choice is yours. You can take control over your attitude, or you can let yourself be swayed by outside factors that will leave you on a motivational roller coaster: fired up one day, and down the next. Getting motivated on a given day can sometimes be as simple as saying a few key words and taking a walk. But staying motivated requires a strategy or motivational training program. To understand the process, we must first look inside your head.

The brain has two hemispheres that are separated and don't interconnect. The logical left brain does our business activities, trying to steer us into pleasure and away from discomfort. The creative and intuitive right side is an unlimited source of solutions to problems and connects us to hidden strengths.

As we accumulate stress, the left brain sends us a stream of logical messages that tell us, "Slow down", "Stop and you'll feel better", "This isn't your day", and even philosophical messages like "Why are you doing this?" We are all capable of staying on track, and maintaining motivation even when the left brain is saying these things. So, the first important step in taking command over motivation is to ignore the left brain unless there is a legitimate reason of health or safety (very rare). You can deal with the left brain through a series of mental training drills.

These drills allow the right side of the brain to work on solutions to the problems you are having. As the negative messages spew out of the left brain, the right brain doesn't argue. By preparing mentally for the challenges you expect, you will be empowered to deal with the problems and to develop mental toughness. But even more important, you will have three strategies for success.

Drill #1
Rehearsing success

Getting out the door after a hard day

By rehearsing yourself through a motivation problem, you can be more consistent and set the stage to improve. You must first have a goal that is do-able, and a rehearsal situation that is realistic. Let's learn by doing:

1. State your desired outcome: To be walking and running from my house after a hard day.

2. Detail the challenge: Low blood sugar and fatigue, a stream of negative messages, need to get the evening meal ready to be cooked, overwhelming desire to feel relaxed.

3. Break up the challenge into a series of actions, which lead you through the mental barriers, not one of which is challenging to the left brain.

- You're driving home at the end of the day, knowing that it is your exercise day but you have no energy.
- Your left brain says, "You're too tired", "Take the day off", "You don't have the energy to run-walk."
- So you say to the left brain, "I'm not going to exercise. I'll put on some comfortable shoes and clothes, eat and drink, get food preparation going for dinner, and feel relaxed."
- You're in your room, putting on comfortable clothes and shoes (they just happen to be used for run-walk).
- You're drinking coffee (tea, diet cola, etc.) and eating a

good tasting energy snack, as you get the food prepared to go into the oven.

- Stepping outside, you check on the weather.
- You're walking out to the edge of your block to see what the neighbors are doing.
- As you cross the street, you're on your way.
- The endorphins are kicking in, you feel good; you want to continue.

4. Rehearse the situation over and over, fine-tuning it so that it becomes integrated into the way you think and act.

5. Finish by mentally enjoying the good feelings experienced with the desired outcome. You have felt the good attitude, the vitality, the glow from a good run-walk, and you are truly relaxed. So, revisit these positive feelings at the end of each rehearsal.

Getting out the door early in the morning

The second most common motivational problem that I'm asked about relates to the comfort of the bed when you wake up and know that it is time for exercise.

State your desired outcome: to be walking and running away from the house early in the morning.

Detail the challenge: a desire to lie in bed, no desire to exert yourself so early. The stress of the alarm clock, and having to think about what to do next when the brain isn't working very fast is challenging.

Break up the challenge into a series of actions, which lead you through the mental barriers, not one of which is challenging to the left brain.

- The night before, lay out your running clothes and shoes near your coffee pot, so that you don't have to think.
- Set your alarm, and say to yourself over and over, "feet on the floor, alarm off, to the coffee pot." Or...."floor, alarm, coffee." As you repeat this, you visualize doing each action without thinking. By repeating it, you lull yourself to sleep. You have been programming yourself for taking action the next morning.
- The alarm goes off. You put the feet on the floor, shut the alarm off, and head to the coffee pot—all without thinking.
- You're putting on one piece of clothing at a time, sipping coffee, never thinking about exercise.
- With coffee cup in hand, you walk out the door to see what the weather is like.
- Sipping coffee, you walk to edge of your block or property to see what the neighbors are doing.
- Putting coffee down, you cross the street, and you have made the break!
- The endorphins are kicking in; "you feel good", you want to continue.

Rehearsals become patterns of behavior more easily if you don't think, but just move from one action to the next. The power of the rehearsal is that you have formatted your brain

for a series of actions, so that you don't have to think as you move from one action to the next. As you repeat the pattern, revising it for real life, you become what you want to be.

You are successful!

Drill # 2
Magic words

Even the most motivated person has sections during a tough exercise session when they want to quit. By using a successful brainwashing technique, you can pull yourself through these negative thoughts, and feel so good at the end. On these days, you have not only reached the finish line—you've overcome challenges to get there. Here's how it works.

Each of us have characteristic problems that keep on coming back. These are the ones that we can also expect to bother us in the future. Go back in your memory bank and pull out instances when you started to lose motivation due to these, but finished and overcame the challenge.

Relax.......Power.......Glide

In really tough runs, I have three such challenges: 1) I become tense when I get really tired, worried that I will struggle badly at the end. 2) I feel the loss of the bounce and strength I had at the beginning, and worry that there will be no strength at the end. 3) My form starts to get ragged, and I worry about further deterioration of muscles and tendons and more fatigue due to "wobbling."

Over the past three decades I have learned to counter these three problems with the magic words "Relax... Power.... Glide." The visualization of each of these positives helps a little. The real magic comes from the association I have made with hundreds of situations when I started to "lose it" in one of the three areas, but overcame the problems.

CROSS TRAINING:
EXERCISE YOU CAN DO ON THE NON-RUNNING DAYS

My run-walk method has helped tens of thousands of new runners avoid injury while they enjoy the increased vitality and attitude that comes with regular running. A growing percentage of these new runners have had such a good experience with running injury free that they think they are immune to aches and pains. They are wrong.

Too much of a good thing

The hard work of running involves lifting your body off the ground, and then absorbing the shock. If you are doing this every other day, the limited damage can be repaired, and your fitness improved. Many runners—even in their 50s and 60s—don't ever have problems.

Once runners get into a regular running routine, and enjoy the vitality and attitude boost, some will try to sneak in an extra day or two on the days they should be off. The same people that had trouble getting motivated for months, suddenly get out of control, and suffer from aches and pains.

The logic goes like this: if the minimal amount of running made them feel pretty good, then increasing the mileage will make them feel much better. By adding one or two extra running days, the injury risk doubles or triples.

Cross training activities

The middle ground is to run one day, and cross train the next. Cross training simply means "alternative exercise" to running. Your goal is to find exercises that give you the same type of boost as you receive from running, but without tiring the workhorses of running: calf muscles, Achilles tendon, hamstring.

The other exercises may not deliver the same good feelings—but they can come close. Many runners report that it may take a combination of 3 or 4 in a session to do this.

But even if you don't feel exactly the same way, you'll receive the relaxation that comes from exercise, burn calories and fat.

When you are starting to do any exercise (or starting after a layoff):

1. Start with 5 easy minutes of exercise, rest for 20 or more minutes, and do 5 more easy minutes.
2. Take a day of rest after this exercise (you can do another exercise the next day).
3. Increase by 2-3 additional minutes each session until you get to the number of minutes that you feel comfortable doing.
4. Once you have reached two 15 minute sessions, you could shift to one 22-25 minute session, and increase by 2-3 more minutes per session if you wish.
5. It's best to do no exercise the day before a long run.
6. To maintain your conditioning in each exercise, it's best to do one session a week of 10 minutes or more once your reach that amount.
7. The maximum cross training is up to the individual. As long as you are feeling fine for the rest of the day, and having no trouble with your runs, the length of your cross training should not be a problem.

Water running can improve your running form

All of us have little flips and side motions of our legs that interfere with our running efficiency. The resistance of the water forces your legs to find a more efficient path. In addition, several leg muscles are strengthened which can help to keep your legs on a smoother path when they get tired at the end of a long run.

Here's how!

You'll need a flotation belt for this exercise. The product "aqua jogger" is designed to float you off the bottom of the pool, and on most runners, tightens so that it is close to the body. There are many other ways to keep you floating, including simple water ski float belts and life jackets.

Get in the deep end of the pool and move your legs through a running motion: little or no knee lift, kicking out slightly in front of you, and bringing the leg behind, with the foot coming up, so that the lower and upper leg make a 90 degree angle behind you. As in running, your lower leg should be parallel with the horizontal.

If you are not feeling much exertion, you're probably lifting the knees too high, and moving your legs through a tiny range of motion. To get the benefit, an extended running motion is needed.

It's important to do water running once a week to keep the adaptations that you have gained. If you miss a week, you should drop back a few minutes from your previous session. If you miss more than 3 weeks, start back at two 5-8 minutes sessions.

Fat burning and overall fitness exercises

Nordic Track

This exercise machine simulates the motion used in cross country skiing. It is one of the better cross training modes for fat burning because it allows you to use a large number of muscle cells while raising body temperature. If you exercise at an easy pace, you can get into the fat burning zone (past 45 minutes) after a gradual build up to that amount.

This exercise requires no pounding of the legs or feet and (unless you push it too hard or too long) allows you to run as usual the next day.

Rowing machine

There are a number of different types of rowing machines. Some work the legs a bit too hard for runners, but most allow you to use a wide variety of lower and upper body muscle groups.

Like Nordic track, if you have the right machine for you, it's possible to continue to exercise for about as long as you wish, once you have gradually worked up to this. Most of the better machines will use a large number of muscle cells, raise temperature, and can be continued for more than three-quarters of an hour.

Cycling

Indoor cycling (on an exercise cycle) is a better fat burner exercise than outdoor cycling because it raises your body temperature. The muscles used in both indoor and outdoor cycling are mostly the quadraceps muscles—on the front of the upper thigh—reducing the total number of muscle cells compared with other modes.

Don't forget walking!

Walking can be done all day long. I call walking a "stealth fat-burner" exercise because it is so easy to walk mile after mile—especially in small doses. But, it is also an excellent cross training exercise; this includes walking on the treadmill.

Cross training for the upper body

Weight training

While weight work is not a great fat-burning exercise, and does not directly benefit running, it can be done on non-running days, or on running days (after a run).

There are a wide range of different ways to build strength. If interested, find a coach that can help you build strength in the muscle groups you wish. As mentioned previously in this book, weight training for the legs is not recommended.

Swimming

While not a fat-burner, swimming strengthens the upper body while improving cardiovascular fitness and endurance in those muscles. Swimming can be done on both running days and non-running days.

Don't do these on non-running days!

The following exercises will tire the muscles used for running, and keep them from recovering between run days. If you really like to do any of these exercises, you can do them after a run on a running day.

- Stair machines
- Stair aerobics
- Weight training for the leg muscles
- Power walking—especially on a hilly course
- Spinning classes (on a bicycle) in which you get out of your seat

DEALING
WITH THE WEATHER

"Neither rain, nor ice, nor heat, nor gloom nor night shall keep us from our run."

Sometimes, on those snowy, rainy, brutally cold days, I yearn for the early days of running when we had an excuse for not braving the elements. Today, however, there are garments for each of the above, head to toe. Yes, technology has taken away most of our excuses for not exercising. But runners can be very creative. Every year I hear a few new excuses from runners who rise to the occasion and find some reason why they can't exercise. In reality, even if you don't have the clothing for hot or cold weather, you can run/walk indoors—on treadmills, in malls or stadiums, or at a gym.

A few years ago, I ran a race in Fairbanks Alaska. I had to ask the members of the local running club what was the lowest temperature that anyone had endured. The winner had run a 10K in minus 66°F degree weather (not wind-chill; this was the real thing: bulb temperature). He said that it really didn't feel that cold. The fact is that clothing designers have responded to the needs of runners during extreme weather conditions, making it possible to run, fairly comfortably, in sub zero conditions. I will admit, however, that if it is minus 66, I can't run because I have to rearrange my running shoes next to a warm fire.

Hot weather

I've heard rumors of an air conditioned suit for the heat, but haven't seen it offered by the clothing manufacturers. I could have used this when I ran a marathon in Key West, FL. when it was 95°F degrees for the last 20 miles of the race. After decades of running in hot weather areas, mostly in Florida and Georgia, with some time spent in Hawaii and the Philippines, I haven't seen much in clothing that lowers body temperature. The best you can hope for is to minimize the rise, while you feel cooler, and a bit more comfortable.

When you exercise strenuously in high heat (above 70°F), or moderate heat (above 60°F) with high humidity (above 50%) you raise your core body temperature. Most beginning runners will see the internal temperature rise above 55°F. This triggers a release of blood into the capilliaries of your skin to help cool you down. But this diversion reduces the blood supply available to your exercising muscles, meaning that you will have less blood and less oxygen delivered to the power source that moves you forward—and less blood to move out the waste products from these work sites.

So the bad news is that in warm weather you are going to feel worse and run slower. If you build up the heat too quickly, stay out too long, or run too fast—for you—the result could be heat disease. Make sure that you read the section on this health problem at the end of this chapter.

The good news is that you can adapt to these conditions to some extent as you learn the best time of the day, clothing, and other tricks to keep you cool. But there are some other good options below, so read on.

Running through the summer heat

1. Run before the sun gets above the horizon. Get up early during warm weather, and you will avoid most of the dramatic stress from the sun. This is particularly a problem in humid areas. Early morning is usually the coolest time of the day, also. Without having to deal with the sun, most runners can gradually adapt to heat. At the very least, your runs will be more enjoyable. Note: be sure to take care of safety issues.

2. If you must run when the sun is up, pick a shady course. Shade provides a significant relief in areas of low humidity, and some relief in humid environments.

3. Evening and night running is usually cooler in areas with low humidity. In humid environments, there may not be much relief.

4. Have an indoor facility available. With treadmills, you can exercise in air conditioning. If a treadmill bores you, alternate segments of 5-10 minutes—one segment outdoor, and the next indoor.

5. Don't wear a hat! You lose most of your body heat through the top of your head. Covering the head will cause a quicker internal buildup of heat.

6. Wear light clothing, but not cotton. Many of the new, technical fibers (polypro, coolmax, drifit, etc.) will move moisture away from your skin, producing a cooling effect. Cotton soaks up the sweat, making the garment heavier and hotter.

7. Pour water over your head. Evaporation not only helps the cooling process—it makes you feel cooler. If you can bring along ice water with you, you will feel a lot cooler as you squirt some regularly over the top of your head.

8. Do your run-walk in installments. It is fine, on a hot day, to put in your 30 minutes by doing 10 in the morning, 10 at noon and 10 at night. The long run, however, should be done at one time.

9. Take a pool break, or a shower chill-down. During a run, it really helps to take a 2-4 minute dip in a pool or a shower. Some runners in hot areas run loops around their neighborhood, and let the hose run over the head each lap. The pool is especially helpful in soaking out excess body temperature.
   I have run in 97°F degree temperatures at our Florida retreat area, breaking up a 5 mile run into 3 x 1.7 mile run. Between each, I take a 2-3 minute "soak break"

and get back out there. It was only at the end of each segment that I got warm again.

10. Sun Screen—be sure to protect yourself. Some products, however, produce a coating on the skin, slowing down the perspiration and causing an increase in body temperature buildup. If you are only in the sun for 10-30 minutes at a time, you may not need to put on sunscreen for cancer protection. Consult with a dermatologist for your specific needs—or find a product that doesn't block the pores.

11. Drink 6-8 oz. of a sports drink like Accelerade or water at least every 2 hours, or when thirsty throughout the day during hot weather.

12. Look at the clothing thermometer at the end of this section. Wear loose fitting garments that have some texture in the fabric. Texture will limit or prevent the perspiration from causing a clinging effect, sticking to the skin.

13. If your only option is going outside on a very hot day, you have my permission to re-arrange your running shoes—preferably in an air conditioned environment.

Hot weather slowdown

As the temperature rises above 55°F, your body starts to build up heat, but most runners aren't significantly slowed until 60°F. If you make the adjustments early, you won't have to suffer later and slow down a lot more at that time. The baseline for this table is 60°F or 14°C.

Between 60°F and 65°F Between 14°C and 17°C	slow down 30 seconds per mile slower than you would run at 60°F slow down 20 seconds per kilometer slower than you would run at 14°C
Between 66°F and 69°F	Slow down one minute per mile slower than you would run at 60°F
Between 18°C and 19°C	slow down 40 seconds per kilometer slower than you would run at 14°C
Between 70°F and 75°F	slow down 1:30/mile slower than you would run at 60°F
Between 19°C and 22°C	slow down one minute/kilometer slower than you would run at 14°C
Between 76°F and 80°F	slow down 2 min./mi. slower than you would run at 60°F
Between 23°C and 25°C	slow down 1:20/km slower than you would run at 14°C
Above 80°F and 25°C	be careful, take extra precautions to avoid heat disease Or....exercise indoors Or....arrange your shoes next to the air conditioner

Heat disease alert !

While it is unlikely that you will push yourself into heat disease, the longer you are exercising in hot (and/or humid) conditions, the more you increase the likelihood of this dangerous medical situation. That's why I recommend breaking up your exercise into short segments when it's hot, and you must run outdoors. Be sensitive to your reactions to the heat, and those of the runners around you. When one of the symptoms is present, this is normally not a major problem unless there is significant distress. But when several are experienced, take action because heat disease can lead to death. It's always better to be conservative: stop the workout and cool off.

Symptoms:

- Intense heat build-up in the head
- General overheating of the body
- Significant headache
- Significant nausea
- General confusion and loss of concentration
- Loss of muscle control
- Excessive sweating and then cessation of sweating
- Clammy skin
- Excessively rapid breathing
- Muscle cramps
- Feeling faint

Risk factors:

- Viral or bacterial infection
- Taking medication—especially cold medicines, diruretics, medicines for diarrhea, antihistamines, atropine, scopolamine, tranquilizers
- Dehydration (especially due to alcohol)
- Severe sunburn

- Overweight
- Lack of heat training
- Exercising more than one is used to
- Occurrence of heat disease in the past
- Several nights of extreme sleep deprivation
- Certain medical conditions including high cholesterol, high blood pressure, extreme stress, asthma, diabetes, epilepsy, drug use (including alcohol), cardiovascular disease, smoking, or a general lack of fitness.

Take action! Call 911

Use your best judgement, but in most cases anyone who exhibits two or more of the symptoms should get into a cool environment, and receive medical attention immediately. An extremely effective cool off method is to soak towels, sheets, or clothing in cool or cold weather, and wrap them around the individual. If ice is available, sprinkle some ice over the wet cloth.

Heat adaptation workout

If you regularly force yourself to deal with body heat buildup, your body will get better at dealing with it. As with all training components, it is important to do this regularly. You should be sweating to some extent at the end of the workout although the amount and the duration of perspiration is an individual issue. If the heat is particularly difficult, cut back the amount.

Important Note: Read the section on heat disease and stop this workout if you sense that you are even beginning to become nauseous, lose concentration or mental awareness of your condition, etc.

- This is done on a short running day once a week.
- Do the run-walk ratio that you usually use, going at a comfortable pace.
- Warm up with a 5 min walk and take a 5 min walk warmdown.
- Temperature should be between 75°F and 85°F (22-27°C) for best results.
- Stop at the first sign of nausea or significant heat stress.
- When less than 70°F (19°C), you can put on additional layers of clothing to simulate a higher temperature.
- First session, run-walk for only 3-4 minutes in the heat.
- Each successive session, add 2-3 minutes.

Tip: Maintaining heat tolerance during the winter

By putting on additional layers of clothing, so that you sweat within 3-4 minutes of your run-walk, you can keep much of your summer heat conditioning that took so much work to produce. Continue to run for a total of 5-12 minutes at an easy pace.

Dealing with the cold

While most of my runs have been in temperatures above 60°F, I've also run in minus 30°F degrees. I prepared for this run extensively and put on about as many layers as I had in my suitcase.

When I met my winter running guide for the run, he quickly evaluated my clothing and found me lacking. After another two layers, I was ready to go.

The specific type of garments, especially the one next to your skin, is an individual issue. I'm not going to get into the specifics here because the technology changes quickly. In general, you want your first layer to be comfortable and not too thick. There are a number of fabrics today, mostly man-made, that hold a comfortable amount of body heat close to the skin to keep you warm, but don't let you overheat. Most of these same fibers allow for moisture such as perspiration and rain, to be moved away from the skin— even as you run and walk.

Not only does this add to your comfort in winter, but almost eliminates a chill due to having wet skin in a cold wind.

Running through the chill of winter

1. Expand your lunch hour if you want to run outdoors. Mid day is usually the warmest time of the day, so you will probably have to plan to arrive at work early (pay bills, run errands, etc.). The mid day sun can make your outdoor running much more comfortable—even when it is very cold.

2. If early morning is the only time you can run, bundle up. The "clothing thermometer" at the end of this section will help you to dress for the temperature and not over-dress.

3. Run into the wind at the start, particularly when you are running out and turning around. If you run with the wind at your back for the first half of the run, you'll tend to sweat. When you turn into a cold wind, you'll chill down dramatically.

4. Having a health club will give you an indoor venue, and other exercise. With treadmills, you can run away from the wind chill. I have worked with many runners who hate running on treadmills, but also hate running for more than 15 minutes in the cold. Their solution is to

alternate segments of 7-15 minutes—one segment outdoor, and the next indoor. Count the transition as a walk break. Health clubs expand your exercise horizons offering a variety of alternative exercise.

5. One of your exercise days could be a Triathlon—your choice of three exercises. You can do exercises out of your home, or at a health club. See the sidebar on "winter triathlon" for more information.

6. Seek out a large indoor facility near your office or home. In Houston, runners use the tunnels below city streets. Many northern cities offer skyways and allow runners and walkers to use them when traffic allows it. Domes, malls and civic centers often allow winter runners and walkers at certain times.

7. Wear a hat! You lose most of your body heat through the top of your head. Covering the head will help you retain body heat and stay warm.

8. Cover your extremities from the wind chill you produce when you run and walk in the cold! Protect ears, and hands, nose and generally the front of the face. Make sure that you protect the feet with socks that are thick enough. And men, wear an extra pair of underwear.

9. Do your run-walk in installments. It is fine, on a really cold day, to put in your 30 minutes by doing 10 in the morning, 10 at noon and 10 at night.

10. Take a "warm up" break. Before you head out into the cold, walk and run in place, indoors. During a run, when you get really cold on outside, it really helps to

take a 2-4 minute walk indoors. Some runners schedule their walk breaks to coincide with buildings that allow public walking.

11. Vasoline—be sure to protect yourself wherever there is exposed skin on very cold days. One area, for example, is the skin around the eyes, not protected by a ski mask, etc.

12. When you are exercising during the winter, indoor or outdoor, you will be losing almost as much in sweat as in the warm months. You should still drink at least 4-6 oz. of a sports drink like Accelerade or water at least every 2 hours, or when thirsty throughout the day.

13. Another reminder: Look at the clothing thermometer at the end of this section, and customize it for your situation.

Winter triathlon

Energize your winter workouts by doing three or more segments during your training. Here's how it works:

1. Select one day a week for your triathlon. Select three activities.
2. Some outdoor activities are run-walk, cross country skiing, skating, snow shoeing, etc.
3. Some indoor health club activities are run-walk, swim, stair machine, exercycle, rowing machine, etc.
4. Some indoor activities at home are exercise machines, stairs, weights, situps, rope skipping, running in place, aerobic video exercise.
5. Alternate the activities for about 5-10 minutes at a time.
6. If desired, keep a log of how much work you do on each machine, miles run, minutes for each activity, etc.

7. Expand to a pentathlon (5 events), decathlon (10 events) or whatever.
8. Combine indoor and outdoor activities if you wish; set up your "world record" list.

Clothing thermometer

After years of working with people in various climates, here are my recommendations for the appropriate clothing based upon the temperature. As always, however, wear what works best for you. The general rule is to choose your garments by function first. And remember that the most important layer for comfort is the one next to your skin. Garments made out of fabric labeled Polypro, coolmax, drifit, etc., hold enough body heat close to you in winter, while releasing extra heat. In summer and winter, they move moisture away from the skin—cooling you in hot weather, and avoiding a chill in the winter.

Temperature	What to wear
14°C or 60°F and above	Tank top or singlet, and shorts
9 to13°C or 50 to 59°F	T-shirt and shorts
5 to 8°C or 40 to 49°F	Long sleeve light weight shirt, shorts or tights (or nylon long pants) Mittens and gloves
0 to 4°C or 30 to 39°F	Long sleeve medium weight shirt, and another T-shirt, tights and shorts, Socks or mittens or gloves, and a hat over the ears

-4 to –1°C or 20-29°F	Medium weight long sleeve shirt, another T-shirt, tights and shorts, socks, mittens or gloves, and a hat over the ears
-8 to –3°C or 10-19°F	Medium weight long sleeve shirt, and medium/heavy weight shirt, Tights and shorts, nylon wind suit, top and pants, socks, thick mittens, and a hat over the ears
-12 to –7°C or 0-9°F	Two medium or heavyweight long sleeve tops, thick tights, Thick underwear (especially for men), Medium to heavy warm up, gloves and thick mittens, ski mask, a hat over the ears, and Vaseline covering any exposed skin.
-18 to –11°C or –15°F 	Two heavyweight long sleeve tops, tights and thick tights, thick underwear (and supporter for men), thick warm up (top and pants) mittens over gloves, thick ski mask, and a hat over ears, vasoline covering any exposed skin, thicker socks on your feet and other foot protection, as needed.
Minus 20° both C & F	Add layers as needed

What not to wear

1. A heavy coat in winter. If the layer is too thick, you'll heat up, sweat excessively, and cool too much when you take it off.
2. No shirt for men in summer. Fabric that holds some of the moisture will give you more of a cooling effect as you run and walk.
3. Too much sun screen—it can interfere with sweating.
4. Socks that are too thick in summer. Your feet swell and the pressure from the socks can increase the chance of a black toenail and blisters.
5. Lime green shirt with bright pink pocka dots (unless you have a lot of confidence and/or can run fast).

DESTROYING EXCUSES

All of us have days when we don't feel like running. On some of those days, you probably need a day off due to too much running, or other physical activity. But usually, this is not the case. The fact is that when we are under stress in life (and who isn't) the left brain will have dozens of great reasons why we shouldn't run. They are all perfectly logical and accurate.

Each of us can choose whether to listen to the excuse or not. Once you quickly decide whether there is a medical (or other legitimate reason) why you shouldn't run, most of the time you'll conclude that the left brain is just trying to make you lazy.

Thinking ahead will not take any significant time away from your day, and will destroy most of these excuses. You'll discover pockets of time, more energy, quality time with kids, and more enjoyment of exercise than you thought were possible for you.

The following is a list of excuses that most of us hear on a regular basis. With each, I've given a strategy for breaking through the excuse. Most of the time, it is as simple as just getting out there. But overall, you are the captain of your ship. If you take charge over your schedule and your attitude, you will plan ahead. As you learn to ignore the left brain, and put one foot in front of the other, the endorphins start flowing, and the excuses start to melt away.

Life is good!

I don't have time to run

Most of the recent US Presidents have been runners, as well as most of their vice presidents. Are you more busy than the President? There are always pockets of time, 5 minutes here, 10 minutes there, when you can insert a walk-run. With planning, you'll find several half hours each day. Many runners find that as they get in better shape, they don't need as much sleep which allows for a chunk of time before the day gets started.

It all gets down to the question "Are you going to take control over the organization of your day or not?" Once you look at your schedule, you'll usually discover other time blocks that allow you to do other things. By making time for a run, you will also tend to be more productive and efficient, more than "paying back" the time you spend running. Bottom line is that you have the time; take it and you will have more quality in your life.

The run will hurt or make me tired

If this happens, you are the one responsible. You have almost complete control over this situation. By going at a conservative pace, with the right amount of running and walking, you will feel better and more energized after the run than before. If you have a bad habit of pushing the pace too much in the beginning, then get control over yourself! Walk more in the beginning, and slow down your running pace. As you learn to slow down, you'll be able to go farther with more energy.

I need to spend some time with my kids

There are a number of running strollers that allow parents to run with their kids. My wife and I logged thousands of miles with our first child in single "baby jogger." We got a twin carrier after our second was born. With the right pacing, you can talk to the kids about anything, and they can't run or crawl away. Sorry, they don't have a model for teenagers. Because we were with the kid(s) in close company, we found that we talked more, and got more feedback than doing other activities together. By bringing them along with you on a run, you become a great role model: even though busy, you take time to exercise and spend time with kids.

I've got too much work to do

There will always be work to do. Several surveys have found that runners get more work done on days they run. Running produces more energy and a better attitude. It reduces stress. Hundreds of runners have told me that the early morning run allowed the time and the mental energy to organize their day better than any other activity. Others said that the after-work run relieved stress, and tied up the mental loose ends from the office. Clearly, you will get as much (probably more) work done each day if you run regularly. It is up to you to take charge, so that you will insert the run into your day.

I don't have the energy to run today

This is one of the easier ones to solve. Most of the runners who've worked with me, and had this excuse, had not been eating enough times a day. I don't mean eating more food. In most cases, the quantity of food is reduced. By eating about every 2-3 hours, most people feel more energized, more of the time. Even if you aren't eating well during the day, you can overcome low blood sugar by having a "booster" snack about an hour before a run. Caffeine helps (as long as you don't have caffeine sensitivities). My dynamic food duo is a PowerBar and a cup of coffee. Just carry some food with you, and energize yourself before a run.

I don't have my running shoes and clothes with me

Take an old bag (backpack, etc.) and load it with a pair of running shoes, a top for both winter and summer, shorts and warmup pants, towel, deodorant, and anything else you would need for a run and clean up. Put the bag next to the front door, or in the trunk of your car, etc. Then, the next time you are waiting to pick up your child from soccer, etc., you can do a quick change in the restroom and make some loops around the field.

I'd rather be sitting on a couch eating candy

Ok, now it's time for your "test." What is your response to this type of message?

WHAT ABOUT KIDS?

Running is a very natural activity for kids—but they will deny this. Just when you want him to stay with you, your son, who chooses video games over exercise any day of the week, takes off down a crowded supermarket aisle or through the mall—zooming away with a big smile on his face.

As you talk with another parent in the carpool line, needing to get home, you see your daughter (who says she hates exercise) chase a friend over and over again with a smile on her face.

So, when running is spontaneous, kids usually do it—in play groups, soccer, recess, in just about any open area with another child. If kids do some running like this, they feel good, and will learn that they can run—that they are runners. While they still may not admit that they like to run, you'll see them doing it when they are given the opportunity.

Structured, competitive running programs for kids are often not positive. I believe this is due to the fact that distance running is an introspective experience. The inner benefits are not understood or appreciated until adulthood.

Sadly, many of the kids who show talent get mentally burned out when they run in competitive groups. The individualized competition puts pressure that few kids are ready to handle.

The most powerful influence on a kid is an example. If you come in from a run saying how good you feel, and how the run changed your attitude for the better, kids will "file this" in their subconscious.

But if you talk about how the knees hurt, the run was tough, how you were about to puke...guess what opinion your kid will develop about running.

Playful chase games have been a very positive way to integrate running into kids' lives. (Go to a park, once a week and do random activities that involve running. As important is the conversation afterward about how good everybody feels, mind and body.)

It also doesn't hurt to have a reward. This could be a movie, a trip to a favorite restaurant, a running shirt, or something silly. The latter is usually as powerful as any of the others.

If you can find a running oriented sport that your child enjoys, he or she will get in shape while meeting athletic friends. Try to choose a team that has a positive coach who gently helps the kids improve skills and makes positive statements to the kids when they respond.

It is also appropriate to criticize kids who are goofing off. (You don't want a coach that uses running as punishment, however). Many runners at the high school and college level got their start in sports through soccer. Soccer kids tend to do a lot of running without realizing it.

My two boys have become collegiate distance runners. More than their achievements is the satisfaction that they receive when they choose to go out and run without someone telling them to do so. Somehow, even with a running-compulsive Dad (and Mom), they got it right.

WHAT IF YOU'RE NOT ENJOYING YOUR RUNNING?

Are you tired when you start your run, or a short distance into the run?

This is often due to low blood sugar level. Eat an energy bar and a cup of coffee (or beverage of your choice) about an hour before your run-walk.

Are you doing your run-walk in the same place, day after day?

If you are stuck running in the same place, break out! Go to a scenic or interesting area at least once a week. Some folks are more motivated running in the city, while others can't wait to run on trails. Whatever area motivates you to run, go there.

Are you exercising at a fairly hard level, more than 3 days a week?

If you are tired or simply unmotivated, you may be hitting a temporary "burnout wall." Drop back to an every-other-day exercise routine until you feel the motivation come back.

Most runners in this position find that they respond better by only doing 10 minutes a session at first. After a week or two, 10 minutes is not enough.

Are you running with a group?

The right group will keep you motivated. As you run, you share stories, jokes...your life. There is something very gutteral about running together that encourages you to be yourself and share with others. You don't want to miss the fun of the group.

Are you running the same distance each day?

If so, vary the distance. Have one long run a week, one short run and one medium run. Variety is the spice of running.

Are you running the same speed each day?

You'll tend to get into a boring rut if every day is the same. On your long run day, go very slow. On your short day, run faster in a few one minute segments than you normally run (don't sprint, just run faster than normal).

There are several variations you can make on your other day. Look at the cadence drill mentioned in this book. Not only will this drill help you run more easily and faster—the 20 second cadence counts will break up a run and give you a purpose.

Do you have a goal?

Look at a schedule of running events in your area, and select a race that you want to finish. If you have run this before, you can also target a time goal. As you write the race date on the calendar, you'll find more purpose to every run.

Have you just finished a long term goal?

When you have trained for a challenging event, over several months, it's normal to have a letdown. You can avoid this by selecting a series of motivational runs (social, scenic, festival races) during the 2 months after your goal has been completed.

Write them down on your calendar, or in your training journal at least a month before your first goal. This creates mental motivation that bridges from one event to the next.

Are you writing down your runs in a training journal?

It's motivational to write down mileage, day after day. Often, after looking back over your log entries, you can find a series of reasons why you are not motivated: ran too much during a month, ran too fast, etc.

Once you get into the habit of "journaling", you'll be energized by noting your mileage success each day—and motivated to avoid writing a zero.

Are you giving yourself rewards every few runs?

A smoothie after a long run, or a pancake breakfast after a group run are two examples of food rewards. Our psyche responds positively to a wide range of reinforcements: social, clothing, equipment, emotional, and spiritual. Here are some examples of reinforcements for the spirit:

After a tough run—
"I had to dig down deep today, but
overcame adversity.
I feel good!"

After a great relaxing run—
"There's no better way to clear the
stress than a run like this."

After your longest run all year—
"I can't believe that I ran so far!"

After finishing a run,
when you didn't think you would—
"I feel so empowered; I can do anything."

After a run that was slower than you wanted—
"I am miles ahead of those on the couch."

TROUBLE SHOOTING

- Coming back after a layoff from running
- It hurts!
- No energy…
- Side Pain
- I feel great one day—but the next day…
- No motivation
- Cramps in my leg muscles
- Upset stomach or Diarrhea
- Headache
- Should I run when I have a cold?
- Street safety
- Dogs
- Heart Disease and Running

How do I start back when I've had time off?

The longer you've been away from running, the slower you must return. I want to warn you now that you will reach a point when you feel totally back in shape—but you are not. Stay with the plan below for your return, and when in doubt, be more conservative. Remember that you are in this for the long run!

Less than 2 weeks off You will feel like you are starting over again, but should come back quickly. Let's say that you were at week # 20, but had to take 10 days off. Start back at week #2 for the first week. If all is well, skip to week # 4 or 5 for the second week. If that works well, gradually transition back to the schedule you were using before you had your layoff over the next 2-3 weeks.

14 days to 29 days off You will also feel like you are starting over again, and it will take longer to get it all back: within about 5-6 weeks you should be back to normal. Use the schedule of your choice (from week # 1) for two weeks. If there are no aches, pains or lingering fatigue, then use the schedule, but skip every other week. After the 5th week, transition back into what you were doing before the layoff.

One month or more off If you have not run for a month or more, start over again, like a beginner. Use one of the three schedules in this book following it exactly (from week # 1) for the first few weeks. After 2-3 weeks, the safest plan is to continue with the schedule.

But if you're having no aches and pains, and no lingering fatigue, you could increase more rapidly by skipping one week out of three. After 2 months of no problems, you could skip every other week if everything is still feeling great.

It hurts!

Is it just a passing ache, or a real injury?

Most of the aches and pains you feel when running will go away within a minute or two. If the pain comes on when running, just walk for an additional 2 minutes, jog a few strides, and walk another 2 minutes.

If the pain comes back after doing this 4 or 5 times, stop running and walk. If the pain goes away when you walk, just walk for the rest of the workout.

Walking pain When the pain stays around when walking, try a very short stride. Walk for a 30-60 seconds. If it still hurts when walking, try sitting down, and massaging the area that hurts if you can. Sit for 2-4 minutes. When you try again to walk, and it still hurts, call it a day; your workout is over.

It's an injury if....you have any of the following:

There's inflammation—swelling in the area.

There's loss of function—the foot, knee, etc. doesn't work correctly.

There's pain—it hurts and keeps hurting or gets worse.

Treatment suggestions:

1. See a doctor who has treated other runners very successfully and wants to get you back on the road or trail.
2. Take at least 2-5 days off from any activity that could irritate it to get the healing started, more if needed.
3. If the area is next to the skin (tendon, foot, etc.), rub a chunk of ice on the area(s)—constantly rubbing for 15 minutes until the area gets numb. Continue to do this for a week after you feel no symptoms. Ice bags and gel ice do no good at all in most cases.

4. If the problem is inside a joint or muscle, call your doctor and ask if you can use prescription strength anti-inflammatory medication. Don't take any medication without a doctor's advice—and follow that advice.

5. If you have a muscle injury, see a veteran sports massage therapist. Try to find one who has a lot of successful experience treating the area where you are injured. The magic fingers and hands can often work wonders.

This is advice from one runner to another. For more info on injuries, treatment, etc. see the "injury free" chapter in this book, and *Galloway's Book On Running* (second edition).

No energy today

There will be a number of days each year when you will not feel like exercising. On most of these, you can turn it around and feel great. Occasionally, you will not be able to do this because of an infection, lingering fatigue, or other physical problems. Here's a list of things that can give you energy. If these actions don't lead you to a run, then read the nutrition sections—particularly the blood sugar chapter in this book—or in *Galloway's Book on Running*.

1. Eat an energy bar, with water or caffeinated beverage, about an hour before the run.

2. Instead of #1, half an hour before exercising, you could drink 100-200 calories of a sports drink that has a mix of 80% simple carbohydrate and 20% protein. The product Accelerade has this already put together.

3. Just walk for 5 minutes away from your house, office, etc., and the energy often kicks in. Forward movement gets the attitude moving, too.

4. One of the prime reasons for no energy is that you didn't re-load within 30 minutes after your last exercise session: 200-300 calories of a mix that is 80% simple carbohydrate and 20% protein (Endurox R4 is the product that has this formulated).

5. Low carb diets will result in low energy to get motivated before a workout, and often no energy to finish the workout.

6. In most cases, it is fine to keep going even if you aren't energetic. But if you sense an infection, see a doctor. If the low energy stays around for several days, see a nutritionist that knows about the special needs of exercisers and/or get some blood work done. This may be due to inadequate iron, B vitamins, energy stores, etc.

Note: if you have any problems with caffeine, don't consume any products containing it. As always, if you sense any health problem, see a doctor.

Side pain

This is very common, and usually has a simple fix. Normally, it is not anything to worry about...it just hurts. This condition is due to 1) the lack of deep breathing, and 2) going a little too fast from the beginning of the run. You can correct #2 easily by walking more at the beginning, and slowing down your running pace.

Deep breathing from the beginning of a run can prevent side pain. This way of inhaling air is performed by diverting the air you breathe into your lower lungs. Also called "belly breathing", this is how we breathe when asleep, and it provides maximum opportunity for oxygen absorption. If you don't deep breathe when you run, and you are not getting the oxygen you need, the side pain will tell you. By slowing down, walking, and breathing deeply for a while, the pain may go away. But sometimes it does not. Most runners just continue to run and walk with the side pain. In 50 years of running and helping others run, I've not seen any lasting negative effect from those who run with a side pain.

Tip: Some runners have found that side pain goes away if they tightly grasp a rock in the hand that is on the side of the pain. Squeeze it for 15 seconds or so. Keep squeezing 3-5 times.

You don't have to take in a maximum breath to perform this technique. Simply breathe a normal breath, but send it to the lower lungs. You know that you have done this if your stomach goes up and down as you inhale and exhale. If your chest goes up and down, you are breathing shallowly.

Note: never breathe in and out rapidly. This can lead to hyperventilation, dizziness, and fainting.

I feel great one day...and not the next

If you can solve this problem, you could become a very wealthy person. There are a few common reasons for this, but there will always be "those days" when the body doesn't seem to work right, or the gravity seems heavier than normal—and you cannot find a reason.

1. **Pushing Through.** In most cases, this is a one-day occurrence. Most runners just put more walking into the mix, and get through it. Before pushing, however, make sure that you don't have a medical reason why you feel bad.

2. **Heat and/or Humidity** will make you feel worse. You will often feel great when the temperature is below 60°F and miserable when 75°F or above.

3. **Low blood sugar** can make any run a bad run. You may feel good at the start and suddenly feel like you have no energy. Every step seems to take a major effort. Read the chapter in this book about this topic.

4. **Low motivation.** Use the rehearsal techniques in the "staying motivated" chapter to get you out the door on a bad day. These have helped numerous runners turn their minds around—even in the middle of a run.

5. **Infection** can leave you feeling lethargic, achy, and unable to run at the same pace that was easy a few days earlier. Check the normal signs (fever, chills, swollen lymph glands, etc.) and at least call your doctor if you suspect something.

6. **Medication and alcohol,** even when taken the day before, can leave a hangover that dampens a workout.

7. **A slower start** can make the difference between a good day and a bad day. When your body is on the edge of fatigue or other stress, it only takes a few seconds too fast per mile, walking and/or running, to push into discomfort or worse.

Cramps in the muscles

At some point, most people who run experience cramps. These muscle contractions usually occur in the feet or the calf muscles, and may come during a run or walk, or they may hit at random. Most commonly, they will occur at night, or when you are sitting around at your desk or watching TV in the afternoon or evening.

Cramps vary in severity. Most are mild, but some can grab so hard that they shut down the muscles and hurt when they seize up. Massage, and a short and gentle movement of the muscle can help to bring most of the cramps around. Odds are that stretching will make the cramp worse, or tear the muscle fibers.

Most cramps are due to overuse—doing more than in the recent past, or continuing to put yourself at your limit, especially in warm weather. Look at the pace and distance of your runs and walks in your training journal to see if you have been running too far, or too fast, or both.

- Continuous running increases cramping. Taking walk breaks more often can reduce or eliminate cramps. Several runners who used to cramp when they ran a minute and walked a minute, stopped cramping with a ratio of run 30 seconds and walk 30-60 seconds.

- During hot weather, a good electrolyte beverage can help to replace the salts that your body loses in sweating. A drink like Accelerade, for example, can help to top off these minerals by drinking 6-8 oz. every 1-2 hours.

- On very long hikes, walks or runs, however, the continuous sweating, especially when drinking a lot of fluid, can push your sodium levels too low and produce muscle cramping. If this happens regularly, a buffered salt tablet has helped greatly: Succeed.

• Many medications, especially those designed to lower cholesterol, have as one of their known side effects muscle cramps. Runners who use medications and cramp should ask their doctor if there are alternatives.

Here are several ways of dealing with cramps:

1. Take a longer and more gentle warmup.
2. Shorten your run segment.
3. Slow down your walk, and walk more.
4. Shorten your distance on a hot/humid day.
5. Break your run up into two segments.
6. Look at any other exercise that could be causing the cramps.
7. Take a buffered salt tablet at the beginning of your exercise.

Note: if you have high blood pressure, ask your doctor before taking any salt product.

Upset stomach or diarrhea

Sooner or later, virtually every runner has at least one episode with nausea or diarrhea. It comes from the buildup of total stress that you accumulate. Most commonly, it is the stress of running on that day due to the causes listed below.

But stress is the result of many unique conditions within the individual. Your body triggers the nausea/diarrhea to get you to reduce the exercise, which will reduce the stress. Here are the common causes:

1. **Running too fast or too far** is the most common cause. Runners are confused about this because the pace doesn't feel too fast in the beginning. Each person has a level of fatigue that triggers these conditions. Slowing down and taking more walk breaks will help you manage the problem.

2. **Eating too much or too soon before the run.** Your system has to work hard running, and works hard to digest food. Doing both at the same time raises stress and results in nausea, etc. Having food in your stomach, in the process of being digested, is an extra stress and a likely target for elimination.

3. **Eating a high fat or high protein diet.** Even one meal that has over 50% of the calories in fat or protein can lead to N/D hours later.

4. **Eating too much the afternoon or evening** of the day before. A big evening meal will still be in the gut the next morning, being digested. When you bounce up and down on a run, which you will, you add stress to the system and results in nausea/diarrhea (N/D).

5. **Heat and humidity** are a major cause of these problems. Some people don't adapt to heat well and experience N/D with minimal buildup of temperature or humidity. But in hot conditions, everyone has a core body temperature increase that will result in significant stress to the system—often causing nausea, and sometimes diarrhea. By slowing down, taking more walk breaks, and pouring water over your head, you can manage this better.

6. **Drinking too much water before a run.** If you have too much water in your stomach, and you are bouncing around, you put stress on the digestive system. Reduce your intake to the bare minimum. Most runners don't need to drink any fluid before a run that is 60 minutes or less.

7. **Drinking too much of a sugar/electrolyte drink.** Water is the easiest substance for the body to process. The addition of sugar and/or electrolyte minerals, as in a sports drink, makes the substance harder to digest. During a run (especially on a hot day) it is best to drink only water. Cold water is best.

8. **Drinking too much fluid too soon after a run.** Even if you are very thirsty, don't gulp down large quantities of any fluid. Try to drink no more than 6-8 oz., every 20 minutes or so. If you are particularly prone to this N/D, just take 2-4 sips, every 5 minutes or so. When the body is very stressed and tired, it's not a good idea to consume a sugar drink. The extra stress of digesting the sugar can lead to problems.

9. **Don't let running be stressful to you.** Some runners get too obsessed about getting their run in or running at a specific pace. This adds stress to your life. Relax and let your run diffuse some of the other tensions in your life.

Headache

There are several reasons why runners get headaches on runs. While uncommon, they happen to the average runner about 1-5 times a year. The extra stress that running puts on the body can trigger a headache on a tough day—even considering the relaxation that comes from the run. Many runners find that a dose of an over-the-counter headache medication takes care of the problem. As always, consult with your doctor about use of medication. Here are the causes/solutions.

Dehydration—if you run in the morning, make sure that you hydrate well the day before. Avoid alcohol if you run in the mornings and have headaches. Also watch the salt in your dinner meal the night before. A good sports drink like Accelerade, taken throughout the day the day before, will help to keep your fluid levels and your electrolytes "topped off." If you run in the afternoon, follow the same advice leading up to your run, on the day of the run.

Medications can often produce dehydration—There are some medications that make runners more prone to headaches. Check with your doctor.

Too hot for you—run at a cooler time of the day (usually in the morning before the sun gets above the horizon). When on a hot run, pour water over your head.

Running a little too fast—start all runs more slowly; walk more during the first half of the run

Running further than you have run in the recent past—monitor your mileage and don't increase more than about 15% further than you have run on any single run in the past week.

Low blood sugar level—be sure that you boost your BLS with a snack, about 30-60 minutes before you run. If you are used to having it, caffeine in a beverage can sometimes help this situation also.

If prone to migraines—generally avoid caffeine, and try your best to avoid dehydration. Talk to your doctor about other possibilities.

Watch your neck and lower back—If you have a slight forward lean as you run, you can put pressure on the spine—particularly in the neck and lower back. Read the form chapter in this book and run upright.

Should I run when I have a cold?

There are so many individual health issues with a cold that you must talk with a doctor before you exercise when you have an infection.

Lung infection—don't run! A virus in the lungs can move into the heart and kill you. Lung infections are usually indicated by coughing.

Common Cold? There are many infections that initially seem to be a normal cold, but are not. At least call your doctor's office to get clearance before running. Be sure to explain how much you are running, and what, if any medication you are taking.

Throat infection and above—most runners will be given the OK, but check with the doctor.

Street safety

Each year several runners are hit by cars when running. Most of these are preventable. Here are the primary reasons, and what you can do about them.

1. The driver is intoxicated or preoccupied by cellphone, etc.

Always be on guard—even when running on the sidewalk

or pedestrian trail. Many of the fatal crashes occurred when the driver lost control of the car, and came up behind the runner on the wrong side of the road. I know it is wonderful to be on "cruise control" in your right brain, but you can avoid a life threatening situation if you will just keep looking around, and anticipate.

2. The runner dashes across an intersection against the traffic light

When running or walking with another person, don't try to follow blindly across an intersection. Runners who quickly sprint across the street without looking are often surprised by cars coming from unexpected directions. The best rule is the one that you heard as a child: when you get to an intersection, stop, see what the traffic situation is. Look both ways, and look both ways again (and again) before crossing. Have an option to bail out of the crossing if a car surprises you from any direction.

3. Sometimes, runners wander out into the street as they talk and run

One of the very positive aspects of running becomes a negative one, in this case. Yes, chat and enjoy time with your friends. But every runner in a group needs to be responsible for his or her own safety, footing, etc. The biggest mistake I see is that the runners at the back of a group assume that they don't have to be concerned about traffic at all. This lack of concern is a very risky situation.

- In general, be ready to save yourself from a variety of traffic problems by following the rules below and any other that apply to specific situations. Even though the rules below seem obvious, many runners get hit by cars each year by ignoring them.

- Be constantly aware of vehicular traffic at all times.
- Assume that all drivers are drunk or crazy or both. When you see a strange movement by a car, be ready to get out of the way.
- Mentally practice running for safety. Get into the practice of thinking ahead at all times with a plan for that current stretch of road.
- Run as far off the road as you can. If possible, run on a sidewalk or pedestrian trail.
- Run facing traffic. A high percentage of traffic deaths come from those who run with the flow of traffic, and do not see the threat from behind.
- Wear reflective gear at night. I've heard the accounts and this apparel has saved lives.
- Take control over your safety you are the only one on the road who will usually save yourself.

Dogs

When you enter a dog's territory, you may be in for a confrontation. Here are my suggestions for dealing with your "dog days":

1. There are several good devices that will help deter dogs: an old fashioned stick, rocks, some electronic signal devices, and pepper spray. If you are in a new area, or an area of known dogs, I recommend that you have one of these at all times.

2. At the first sign of a dog ahead, or barking, try to figure out where the dog is located, whether the dog is a real threat, and what territory the dog is guarding.

3. The best option is to run a different route.

4. If you really want or need to run past the dog, pick up a rock if you don't have another anti-dog device.

5. Watch the tail. If the tail does not wag, beware.

6. As you approach the dog, it is natural for the dog to bark and head toward you. Raise your rock as if you will throw it at the dog. In my experience, the dog withdraws about 90% of the time. You may need to do this several times before getting through the dog's territory. Keep your arms up.

7. In a few cases, you will need to throw the rock, and sometimes another if the dog keeps coming.

8. In less that 1% of the hundreds of dog confrontations I've had, there is something wrong with the dog, and it continues to move toward you. Usually the hair will be up on the dog's back. Try to find a barrier to get behind, yell loudly in hopes that the owner or someone will help you. If a car comes by, try to flag down the driver, and either stay behind the car as you get out of the dog's territory, or get in the car for protection if that is appropriate.

9. Develop your own voice. Some use a deep commanding voice, some use a high pitched voice. Whichever you use, exude confidence and command.

TROUBLE SHOOTING ACHES AND PAINS

At the first sign of soreness or irritation in these areas, read the injury chapter. It is always better to take 2-3 days off from running, and then start back making some form adjustments. In most of these areas, I've found that stretching aggravates the problem. For more information, see *Galloway's Book on Running*.

Shins: Soreness or pain in the front of the shin (anterior tibial area)

Note: Even after you make the corrections, shin problems often take several weeks to heal. As long as the shin problem is not a stress fracture, easy running can often allow it to heal as quickly (or more quickly) than complete layoff. In general, most runners can run when they have shin splints; they just need to stay below the threshold of further irritation.

Causes:

1. Increasing too rapidly—just walk for 1-2 weeks, and walk with a short stride, gently.
2. Running too fast, even on one day—when in doubt, run slower and walk slower on all runs.
3. Running or walking with a stride that is too long—shorten stride and use more of a "shuffle."

Soreness or pain at the inside of the lower leg (posterior tibial area)

Causes:

1. Same three causes as in anterior tibial shin splints, see above.
2. More common with runners who over-pronate; this means that they tend to roll to the inside of the foot as they push off.
3. Shoes may be too soft allowing a floppy/pronated foot to roll inward more than usual.

Corrections:

1. Reduce stride length.
2. Put more walking into your run-walk ratio from the beginning.
3. If you are an over-pronator on the forward part of your feet, get a stable, motion control shoe.
4. Ask your foot doctor if there is a foot device that can help you.

Shoulder and neck muscles tired and tight

Primary causes:

You are leaning too far forward as you run.

Other causes:

1. You're holding arms too far away from the body as you run.
2. You're swinging arms and shoulders too much as you run.

Corrections:

1. Use the "puppet on a string" image (detailed in the running form chapter above) about every 4-5 minutes during all runs and walks—particularly the longer ones. This is noted above in the section on posture.
2. Watch how you are holding your arms. Try to keep the arms close to the body.
3. Minimize the swing of your arms. Keep the hands close to the body, lightly touching your shirt or the outside of your shorts as your arms swing.

Lower back: Tight, sore, or painful after a run

Causes:

1. You're leaning too far forward as you run.
2. You're having a stride length that is too long for you.

Corrections:

1. Use the "puppet on a string image several times on all runs and walks—-particularly the longer ones. This is noted above in the chapter on running form in the section on posture.
2. Ask a physical therapist whether some strengthening exercise can help.
3. When in doubt, shorten your stride length.
4. For more information, see *Galloway's Book on Running.*

Knee pain at the end of a run

Causes:

1. Stride length could be too long.
2. You're doing too much, too soon.
3. You're not inserting enough walk breaks, regularly from the beginning.
4. When the main running muscles get tired, you will tend to wobble from side to side.

Corrections:

1. Shorten your stride.
2. Stay closer to the ground, using more of a shuffle.
3. Monitor your mileage in a log book, and hold your increase to less than 10% a week.
4. Use more walk breaks during your run.
5. Start at a slower pace.

Behind the knee: pain, tightness, or continued soreness or weakness

Causes:

1. You're stretching.
2. You're over striding—particularly at the end of the run.

Corrections:

1. Don't stretch.
2. Keep your stride length under control.
3. Keep feet low to the ground.

Hamstrings: tightness, soreness, or pain

Causes:

1. It occurs due to stretching.
2. Stride length is too long.
3. You're lifting the foot too high behind, as your leg swings back.

Corrections:

1. Don't stretch.
2. Maintain a short stride, keeping the hamstring relaxed—especially at the end of the run.
3. Take more walking early in the run, possibly throughout the run.
4. As the leg swings behind you, let the lower leg rise no higher than a position that is parallel to the horizontal before swinging forward again.
5. Deep tissue massage can sometimes help with this muscle group.

Quadraceps (front of the thigh): sore, tired, painful

Causes:

1. This is due to lifting your knee too high—especially when tired.
2. This occurs when using the quads to slow down going downhill because you were running too fast.

Corrections:

1. Maintain little or no knee lift—especially at the end of your run.
2. Run with a shuffle.

3. Let your stride get very short at the top of hills, and when tired—don't lengthen it.
4. If you are running too fast going down hills, keep shortening your stride until you slow down, and/or take more walk breaks on the downhill.

Sore feet or lower legs

Causes:
1. There is too much bounce.
2. You're pushing off too hard.
3. Your shoes don't fit correctly or are too worn out.
4. The insole of your shoe is worn out.

Corrections:
1. Keep feet low to the ground.
2. Maintain a light touch of the feet.
3. Get a shoe check to see if your shoes are too worn.
4. You may need only a new insole.

RUNNING AFTER 40, 50, 60, 70

Every year I hear dozens of people tell me that they wish they could run, but they didn't start doing it when they were younger—and feel it is too late for them. Within a few minutes, these folks wish they hadn't said what they said—to me. I tell them that I work with hundreds of people every year who are in their 40s, 50s, 60s, 70s and even 80s who are taking their first steps. Most of these folks become runners within 6 months. Many of them finish marathons—yes, even the 80 year olds—within a year.

The principles of training which are described in this book apply to everyone—at any age. If you add a little stress followed by rest for recovery, your body rebuilds stronger.

The psychological rewards are the same at any age. Endorphins make your muscles feel better. You have a better attitude all day after a run. Each run brings a special relaxation not bestowed by other activities.

Elliott Galloway

As my father got more obese in his 40s, and more out of shape, he gave me every excuse possible why he couldn't exercise. By his 50th birthday, even I had pretty much given up on trying to get him to exert himself. His "reality check" was a high school reunion.

Out of 25 guys who had been on his football team, only 12 were alive at age 52. As he drove home, the advice of his doctor and others came back to him. He realized that he could be the next to depart this world at a time that he was just getting into his life's work—the founding of an innovative school.

The former all-state athlete was shocked on his first run when he could only run about 100 yards before his legs gave out on him. But he stuck with it. Every other day his mission was to run to one more telephone pole before walking back.

Within a year, he was regularly running around the golf course in front of his office, 3 miles. A year after that, he completed The Peachtree Road Race 10K.

After another 3 years training, he completed a marathon. I'm most proud of the fact that in his mid 80s, my Dad is still walking and running over 20 miles a week.

Today I work with dozens of runners who consider themselves "over the hill." Even the 80+ year old beginners get caught up in the excitement of getting more fit. They cannot believe how much better they feel—every day. Honestly, these people are my heroes. I hope I can be like them when I grow up.

Recovery slows down after 40

Having run since I was 13, I've noticed subtle changes that are usually not noticeable. It's only when I now look back over almost 5 decades of running that I see the trends and the cruel facts.

1. Your recovery rate slows down each year past the age of 40.
2. At the same time, your mental focus has increased, so you can push yourself further into fatigue.
3. By the age of 55, there has been a significant slowdown from the age of 40.
4. By the age of 65, another significant slowdown has occurred—even from 55.
5. Continuing to train the same way every year will produce injuries, lingering fatigue or burnout.
6. It takes longer to warm up for each run.
7. Any type of fast running, for you, will greatly increase the time needed for recovery.

My experience: walk breaks, slower pace

I began to notice increasing and continuous leg fatigue as I approached my 40th birthday when I was running 6-7 days a week. So I decided to follow the advice I was giving to other 40+ runners who felt the same way: run every other day. In about 4 weeks, my legs were fresh again. But after 2 years of getting in only 3 runs a week, I needed more endorphins; I wanted to run more. Gradually, I added more days. Now, at 60, I'm back to running about every day.

How is it then that I enjoy running more now than ever, even when running each day? It's because I am running much slower and taking walk breaks very frequently. At the start of every run, I take a walk break about every minute.

After about 3 miles, I'm usually walking about every 3-4 minutes, but sometimes still at one minute. I adjust for how my body feels that day.

How many days per week should you run?

I am not advocating that you try to run as many days as I do. After about 50 years of running, I've discovered many intuitive tricks, and haven't had a single over-use injury in over 25 years. Feel free to follow that part of my example.

Running fewer days per week has been a great way to reduce injury risk while maintaining conditioning through the decades. Even when runners maintain the same weekly mileage, they reduce injury risk by running fewer days per week.

Adjusting your running days per week by age

If you are experiencing more injuries, fatigue, or less enjoyment, run fewer days.

Below 35 years old	36-45 years old	46-55 years old	56-65 years old	66-75 years old	76 + years old
No more than 5 days	4 days	every other day	3 days	2 run/ 2 walk	2 run/ 1 walk

What do you want out of your running?

This is the most important question for anyone to answer—but especially for runners over 40. For me, the answer is simple—I want to be able to run almost every day, injury-free, for the rest of my life. That is why I slow down and walk often. My ego has been able to adjust to slower running, and I know that I feel better every day because I run slowly.

As I mentioned in the first chapter, you are the captain of your running ship. If you want to run a certain distance every run, or not run slower than a certain pace, or win your age group in the local road races, it is your right to go for it. But have the phone numbers of your sports medicine doctors handy.

But for each goal, you must take responsibility for the consequences. In other words, if you get injured by trying to stay up with a runner or group that is faster than you, realize that you put this on yourself.

You have lots of choices as to what you want to see as your final running product, each day and each year. Think carefully and structure accordingly.

A series of little things...

One of the cruel hoaxes that the body plays on us is that even in our 60s we can come very close to the workouts we did when we were in our 30s. Unfortunately, the recovery time required after these power workouts is substantial, compared with the way it was 30 years ago.

- Making a "social run" into a race. It is too easy to get led astray when we are feeling good. Older runners will often find that their running cadence and stride mechanics can feel easy at the beginning of a run, and sometimes at the end. But the next day, and the day after, it is a different story.
- Trying to run no slower than a certain time produces great fatigue on warm days, hilly courses, etc. Mind games work against us as we get older. Your mind can remember when a certain pace was easy, and will get you focused to stay on track for that goal. It is better to be flexible with distance, pace, course, and weather.

- Junk miles are short runs on days that would be better spent as no-running recovery days. In almost every case it is better to take the day off on a short mileage day—and add the miles to other running days that week.
- Starting runs too fast—even a few seconds per mile—produces much greater fatigue. Your legs will feel so much better if you run slower than you could run, during the first 2-3 miles of a run.
- Over stretching tears muscle and tendon fibers and increases healing time for all runners. This damage takes longer to repair as you get older. It doesn't take much of a stretch to be an over-stretch. Since I've found stretching to be of no benefit for almost all runners I've worked with, I don't recommend it. If you like to stretch, be very careful.
- Pushing beyond your speed or endurance limit for a mile or more will greatly increase the time needed for recovery. Even younger runners must pay for these violations. Older runners pay by not having legs that are bouncy and resilient for a significant period after pushing too hard.
- Running form violations produce more fatigue and muscle damage as we age:
-striding too long
-bouncing too high off the ground (even half an inch too high)
-kicking behind you too far.
Refusing to take walk breaks more often because it is too "wimpy." I'm proud to be a wimpy runner who runs every day—instead of being forced to be a couch sitter because of never taking a walk break.

BEING A GOOD COACH

One of the very best ways to consolidate the items you've learned from running is to help someone get started. Not only will you realize how much you have learned from running, you'll find yourself learning the principles of training and running enjoyment better as you explain them to a novice.

But the best part of this experience is the inner satisfaction. You're not only helping people, you're introducing them to an activity that can improve the quality of their lives. In most cases, the novice runners will thank you, periodically, for the rest of your life.

Get them a good textbook—this book

Go over a chapter at a time, starting at the beginning. Highlight the key passages in the book for him or her. You don't have to do this on every chapter, but it really helps to get each novice headed in the right direction.

Make each session enjoyable—especially during the first month

If your coachee is huffing and puffing, slow down and walk more from the beginning of every run. If there is continuing struggle, then stop for that day.

When you suspect even the possibility of low blood sugar, share an energy bar and coffee, tea, diet drink, etc. about 30-45 minutes before the start. Have a reward after each session—especially a snack to reload composed of 80% carbohydrate and 20% protein. On some special occasions, however, it's OK to have a reward snack that may be a little more decadent than usual.

Find interesting areas where you can run—scenic areas, smooth trails

Convenient running routes near work or home are best for busy people, most of the time. But once a week, an excursion to an interesting area can be very rewarding. It's great to have variety, and you should give your coachee some choice.

On each run, have a joke, a juicy story and a controversial issue

This will break the ice, inject some humor, and help to make this a positive bonding experience. With beginners who are having a hard time getting into it, the little humorous items are often appreciated as much as the shoes and clothing.

Don't push too hard, but encourage

One of the most difficult decisions in coaching is whether to push or back off—whether to use a pat on the back or a kick in the butt. In general, it is important that the person get out there and exercise regularly. When motivation is down, just shoot for a minimal amount, every other day. Realize, however, that to really get hooked, the new runner must develop the desire from within.

Rewards work!

After a certain number of weeks, or after reaching a certain level of fitness, surprise with a reward. It doesn't have to be something expensive or exotic. The reward allows the new runner to focus on his or her progress, and feel the satisfaction of steady work paying off.

When your coachee is ready, find a fun race to attend

Races are such positive experiences for new runners when they have a good leader to coach them through the experience calm the anxieties and share the celebration. The new runner will almost always realize that he or she is like most of the runners in the race.

Just having a race date on a calendar will provide the beginner with an identity that will increase motivation.

Tell him or her about your mistakes

When you open up to your new runner with a personal story, the lessons become more powerful.

Don't over-sell running

The benefits are so powerful that almost everyone who stays with it for 6 months will continue. If your coachee is falling asleep during your one hour speech on the benefits of running (and walking), you know that you've stepped over the line. The experience is more powerful than the preaching—and both are part of the process.

Your greatest reward will be an independent runner

Take it as a real compliment that your coachee will need less and less of your guidance. This means that you were an excellent coach, and that he or she can find a new person and enrich another life.

How many years can a runner expect to improve?

Most runners who stay focused continue to improve their running for at least 10 years. A few runners get caught up in running faster, which is the most frustrating part of running.

Even in this area which is influenced by many variables outside the control of the individual, most runners can expect to improve times for about 5 years. Those who stay really focused can keep improving.

Even if you get caught up in time improvement, I suggest that you find several areas of running enjoyment which can continue to enrich your life. You can select events in every state, each continent, every country in Europe, etc.

Have several reunions with your growing number of running friends, 2-4 times a year. Have a family challenge and meet in a city where most of the family wants to visit.

The best form of running improvement comes from inside. My faster times are long gone, but I enjoy my running now more than ever. Practically every day I feel better, work better, think better because I run. It doesn't get any better!

Special Report: Heart Disease and Running

Running tends to have a protective effect from cardiovascular disease. But more runners die of heart disease than any other cause, and are susceptible to the same risk factors as sedentary people. I know of a number of runners who have suffered heart attacks and strokes who probably could have prevented them if they had taken a few simple tests.

Your heart is the most important organ in your body. This short section is offered as a guide to help you take charge over your heart health, the most important organ for longevity, and quality of life. As always, you need to get advice about your individual situation from a cardiologist who knows you and specializes in this area.

Risk Factors—get checked if you have two of these—or one that is serious

- Family History
- Poor lifestyle habits earlier in life
- High fat/high cholesterol diet
- Have smoked—or still smoke
- Obese or severely overweight
- High blood pressure/High cholesterol

Tests

- Stress Test—heart is monitored during a run that gradually increases in difficulty.
- C reactive Protein—has been an indicator of increased risk.
- Heart scan—an electronic scan of the heart which shows calcification, and possible narrowing of arteries.
- Radioactive dye test—very effective in locating specific blockages. Talk to your doctor about this.
- Carotid ultrasound test—helps to prevent stroke.
- Ankle-brachial test—plaque builup in arteries throughout the body.

None of these are fool proof. But by working with your cardiologist, you can increase your chance of living until the muscles just won't propel you further down the road—past the age of 100.

Other books by Jeff Galloway

Testing Yourself, Meyer & Meyer, 2005.
Galloway's Book on Running, Shelter Publications, 2nd Ed., 2002.
New Marathon, Phidippides Pub., 2000.

Photo & Illustration Credits

Cover Design: Jens Vogelsang

Cover Photo: Stefan Eisend

**Back Cover &
Inside Photos:** Polar Electro
Brennan Galloway
Westin Galloway
Gregory Sheats
p.48/49 Sportpressephoto Bongarts

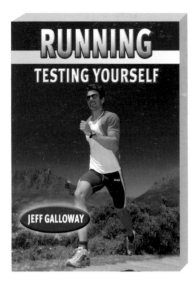

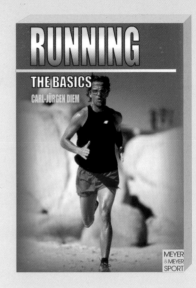

Jeff Galloway
Running
Testing Yourself

For runners and walkers who want to improve, "Running – Testing Yourself" offers programs and practical tips to go farther and faster, while enjoying exercise more than ever.

Inside "Running – Testing Yourself", you'll find specific training programs for fitness test distances used by law enforcement and military organizations.

216 pages, full color print
20 photos, 10 illustrations
Paperback, 5 3/4" x 8 1/4"
ISBN: 1-84126-167-X
c. £ 12.95 UK / $ 17.95 US
$ 26.95 CDN / € 16.95

Carl-Jürgen Diem
Running
The Basics

This book presents the basics of the cardio-vascular system, energy preparation, and the biomechanical aspects of running in a way that is easy to understand.

Advice on clothes, running in different weather conditions and at various times of the day, as well as ideas for compensation exercises, nutrition, injury prevention, etc. complete the contents of this book.

168 pages, full-color print
5 photos, 82 illustrations, 5 tables
Paperback, 5 3/4" x 8 1/4"
ISBN 1-84126-139-4
£ 12.95 UK / $ 17.95 US
$ 25.95 CDN / € 16.90

MEYER & MEYER Sport | sales@m-m-sports.com | www.m-m-sports.com

MEYER & MEYER SPORT

THE BOOK OF
KAREN

Smart Pop is an imprint of BenBella Books, Inc.
10440 N. Central Expressway, Suite 800
Dallas, TX 75231
www.benbellabooks.com
Send feedback to feedback@benbellabooks.com

Printed in the United States of America
10 9 8 7 6 5 4 3 2 1

ISBN 9781953295064 (trade paperback)
ISBN 9781953295453 (ebook)

Editing by Alexa Stevenson

Distributed to the trade by Two Rivers Distribution, an Ingram brand
www.tworiversdistribution.com

**Special discounts for bulk sales are available.
Please contact bulkorders@benbellabooks.com.**